ANDY ALLEN

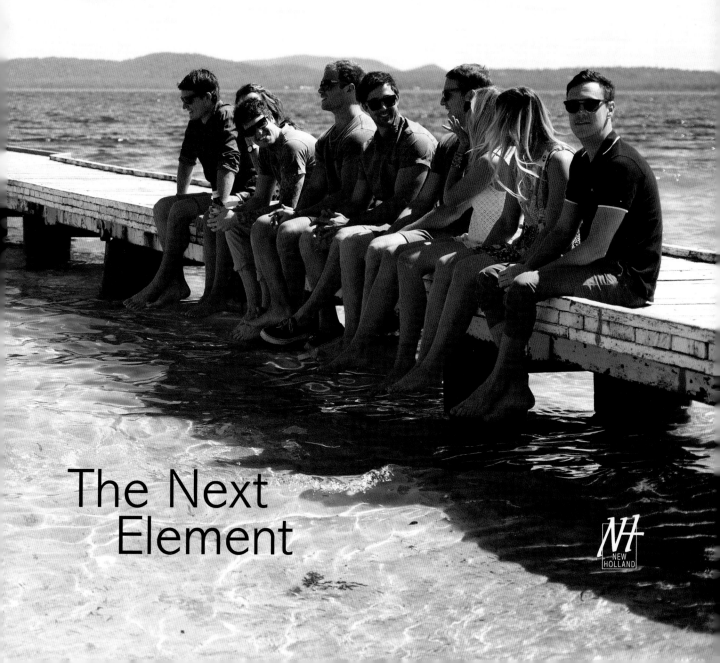

The Next
Element

NH
NEW HOLLAND

CONTENTS

Acknowledgements

I would like to thank the boys from MasterChef 2012 – George Calombaris, Gary Mehigan, Matt Preston and Matt Moran. There is no way I would be where I am today if it wasn't for you guys. Thank you also to everyone behind the scenes in the MasterChef crew.

Thank you to Steve Brown, Bhavani Konings, Janelle Bloom and the team at New Holland for all their help and support.

A special thanks to Kylie Millar for her dessert recipes and friendship.

To Ben Milbourne, a huge thanks for your contribution to my book. There's no way I could have done it without you.

Last but not least, to Mum, Dad, Carly and Philippa. Thanks for always being there for me.

Introduction

After somehow defying the odds and winning the title of MasterChef 2012, I was totally overwhelmed by the challenge of writing my first book. As I worked through the different aspects that were required, I realised how lucky I was, and what an achievement the book would be for me.

The first step was deciding on the title. *The Next Element* reflects the experience I had with the MasterChef competition and the journey I am about to embark upon with food. I feel I have come a long way in a short period of time and it is this which makes me all the more excited about the adventure.

I started out with a basic philosophy about food – keep it simple, but not predictable. However, as my knowledge and experience has grown, I've begun to push the boundaries to create new and exciting flavour combinations.

My Dad was the cook in our family for a long time, but as I became more interested and creative, we started to share the load in the kitchen, until I was on my own, night after night.

After finishing a day's work as an apprentice electrician, I would rush home to prepare the evening meal. This would consist of a tasty classic, to which I would give a 'creative tweak'. This would all have to be done quickly, as I would need to be out the door to go to basketball practice or to meet up with my friends. Everyone should be able to have a crack at the majority of the dishes in the Cooking for My Family section, as at that time, while honing my skills, I was still basically a home cook.

I am incredibly fortunate to have such a close family. I have loved living at home with Mum, Dad and my two sisters, Carly and Philippa.

As Mum and Dad are both school teachers we were lucky enough to have holidays away enjoying ourselves. Initially this was Nambucca Heads, where I have many great memories of fishing and swimming on the beach. In more recent years, we discovered a 'local jewel' in Fingal Bay. My teens were spent around the ocean – swimming, surfing, and spearfishing. I spent my whole holidays immersed in the sea.

Our fishing was restricted to the beach and rocks until Dad bought a boat. We found our catch became more varied, and we spent many afternoons cooking up such delights as whiting, flathead, calamari and Dad's favourite, blue swimmer crabs.

This is where my love for cooking seafood began and which is why you will find many simple seafood dishes in this section.

The next section, Cooking for My Friends, is all about 'share food'. I have them to thank for forcing me to cook in this style, as it was impossible to suggest a sit-down meal to them.

Introduction

To start, it was at afternoon barbecues at whoever's house would be brave enough to have us. Every time we'd have a gathering I took it upon myself to get more creative and not only expand my skills, but educate my mates' palates at the same time. These afternoon barbecues were the massive reason I fell in love with cooking. Food brings the people who are important and special to me together, to have a laugh and enjoy the recipes I create. This is food you can make for four, or easily double the ingredients to cater for a crowd.

If I got nothing more out of MasterChef than the friends and skills I gained from the experience, I'd be a happy man. I also found a new best mate in the MasterChef house, Ben. He and I shared the same interests, not only in food, but also in AFL, basketball and cricket. We helped each other, not only in the kitchen but also with the various day-to-day obstacles we faced. And yes, this 'bromance', is still going strong. I need to give Benny a huge thank you, as without him I would not have had this book on the shelves. Cheers, mate.

While I had many great friends in the house, Kylie is someone who I shared similar interests with. The way her brain works with food is something I envy and I can't wait to see what she does in the future. I now have Kylie to thank for my sister Philippa pumping out macaroons by the dozen, as Kylie was kind enough to pass on her recipe to her.

The third and final section in the book, A New Direction, looks at where I'm going on my food journey since MasterChef. This food reflects how much my cooking changed as a result of being put in some pretty challenging situations and epic experiences.

As you flick through the recipes I encourage you to give them all a go. There's nothing stopping you from accomplishing them all if you read the recipe step by step. After all, that's all I did when I was forced to cook Christine Manfield's, Gaytime Goes Nuts, in the show's finale.

So what's next for me? Everyday, I'm achieving things I would never have dreamed of. Take this book for instance! If you told me a year ago I would be publishing my first book, there is no way that I would have believed you!

I'm continuing to push the boundaries in the kitchen. Ben, Beau, Kylie and I recently decided to take the challenge of creating a pop-up restaurant. We ventured down to Tasmania and set up our Mexican pop-up in the cosy function room at East Devonport Football Club. We catered for 200 people over three nights and I'm happy to say that it was a massive success. I can't wait until we get back together with the crew soon and, who knows, maybe we will be popping up near you…

As a result of spending time with Ben, my new passion is Mexican. I can't wait to travel to Mexico with my buddy and explore the endless food experiences the place has to offer.

I also want to get back to Europe, as during the short time I spent in Italy, my cooking improved dramatically and it is the place where so many great cultures and cuisines exist.

People still ask what type of cook I am, but for me, it's about exploring all the different flavours of the world. I'm not afraid to experiment with flavour combinations, but at the same time, I can't go past a simple backyard seafood barbecue with the people I love. Enjoy!

COOKING FOR MY FAMILY

This section is for every cook who gets home from work and is faced with the dilemma of feeding his or her friends or family. This is where it all began for me. By the time I was 16 I was faced with that challenge on most nights of the week. I had a window from around 5:30pm to 7pm to get dinner on the table. My Dad, who was glad to be out of the kitchen, was sceptical of what I cooked each night, and my two older sisters would laugh at me if everything wasn't spot on. Mum would love every meal no matter what it was, but would complain if it went over the family budget. Although sometimes frustrating, it was all the more satisfying when I ticked all the boxes. During the week, meals were simple – curries and casseroles, meat and three veg – but always with a twist.

On weekends and during the holidays I was able to relax and experiment with the food I served to the family. It began with fishing. From the ripe old age of six, I would catch a few fish with my Dad, which were usually dusted in flour and placed in a frypan. After years of this, I started to experiment with different flavour combinations to take our catch to the next level.

One memory that sticks with me is my Mum's 50th birthday. It was a surprise party at Fingal Bay and Dad and I were lucky enough to spear a few different species of fish to feed the family. I took over the challenge to feed Mum's family. I simply wrapped the fish in foil with some garlic, chilli, ginger, coriander and lemon wedges and baked them in the barbecue. It was a massive hit and it was the first time I felt that buzz of seeing the joy on peoples' faces as they ate my food. I'm happy to say this original recipe made it into this book.

The experiment didn't stop there. I went from boiling a bag of fresh blue swimmer crabs for eight minutes to different variations of chilli crab. My Mum loves oysters and I started to experiment with different flavours to improve the humble, but delicious, oyster.

Sure, there were times when it didn't hit the mark, but for me it was about the times when I got it right and the whole family had a smile from ear to ear.

This is why cooking for the family works for me. It's about bringing the family together, and if you feed them something they love, that's a bonus.

Oysters Kilpatrick

My Mum's favourite.

Serves 4, with 6 oysters each

40ml each of barbecue, worcestershire and
tomato sauce
20ml kecap manis
1 tsp tabasco sauce
1½ tsp garlic, crushed
¼ tsp salt
¼ tsp fresh black pepper
1 cup cheddar cheese, grated
1 cup bacon, diced
2 dozen oysters in their shells
rock salt to serve

Preheat the oven to 180°C.

Mix all the ingredients, except for the oysters, in a bowl.

Place the oysters on a wire rack and top each oyster with 1 heaped teaspoon of the mixture.

Cook for approximately 15 minutes.

To serve, line a dish with rock salt and place the oysters on top.

Mini Egg, Pancetta & Leek Quiches

Makes approximately 16 mini quiches

½ brown onion, finely diced

1 clove garlic, finely diced

1 leek (white part only), finely diced

6 slices pancetta, diced

1 tbs olive oil

salt and pepper to taste

2 thyme sprigs, leaves removed

3 eggs

75ml thickened cream

2 sheets ready-made puff pastry

100g cheddar cheese, grated

fresh chives, to garnish

Preheat oven to 180˚C.

Sauté the onion, garlic, leek, and pancetta in olive oil over a medium heat until the pancetta is crisp and the onions are translucent. Season with salt and pepper to taste.

Add the thyme and sauté until fragrant. Remove from heat and allow to cool.

In a separate bowl, lightly whisk the eggs. Add the cream and mix together.

Lightly grease the holes of a non-stick, shallow muffin tray. Line each hole with puff pastry until it reaches approximately 5cm above the sides of each muffin tin. Prick the base of the pastry with a fork and blind bake in the oven for 10 minutes.

Spoon the onion mixture into the baked pastry cases, until half full, making sure the mixture is evenly distributed. Pour the egg mixture into each pastry case until it just covers the onions.

Top with the grated cheese and bake for 20 minutes, or until the cheese is brown on top. Finish with a sprinkle of chopped chives.

Chilli Blue Swimmer Crab

Brings back memories of my family diving in for the last claw.

Serves 6

3 blue swimmer crabs (or other large crab),
    cleaned and cut into 6 pieces each
2 tbs peanut oil
½ red onion, finely sliced
2 long Thai chillies, finely sliced
2 cloves garlic, finely sliced
2cm piece of ginger, peeled and julienned
2 spring onions, cut into 3cm batons
3 tomatoes, diced
2 tbs dry sherry
1 tbs brown sugar
¼ tbs kecap manis
3 kaffir lime leaves, julienned
1 cup coriander leaves
toasted sourdough or crusty bread to serve

With the back of a knife make a few cracks in the large claws of the crabs.

In a wok over a high heat, add the peanut oil and heat until it starts to smoke.

Add the red onion, chilli, garlic, ginger and spring onions and stir-fry for 1 minute.

Add the crabs and combine for another 30 seconds.

Add the tomatoes, sherry, brown sugar and kecap manis.

Toss everything to combine and then place a lid over the wok and steam the crabs for 5 minutes, depending on the size of the crab, until they are cooked through.

Finish with the kaffir lime leaves, toss for a last time and then serve topped with the coriander leaves and a few pieces of toasted sourdough or crusty bread.

I suggest wearing a bib while you eat!

Simple Chicken Satay

Perfect for a week-night dinner.

Serves 4

1kg chicken thighs, diced into 2cm cubes
juice of 2 limes
2 thyme sprigs, leaves removed
2 tbs black pepper
1 tbs cumin seeds
2 tsp coriander seeds
1 tsp cayenne pepper
2 red chillies, sliced
30g butter
2 red onions, diced
3 cloves garlic, finely chopped
2 cups chicken stock
100g peanut butter, smooth or crunchy
4 tomatoes, deseeded and diced
salt and pepper to taste
coriander and steamed rice, to serve

Marinate the chicken in the lime juice and spices for 30 minutes.

Add the butter to a pan and heat. Sauté the onion and garlic until it is translucent. Add the chicken in batches to the pan, pour in marinade, and cook chicken until it has browned.

Heat the stock in a saucepan. Add peanut butter to the stock and reduce to make a paste. Pour the stock mixture over the chicken pieces and simmer for 15 minutes.

Add the tomatoes and cook for another 5 minutes. Season with salt and pepper and serve with rice and coriander.

Roast Chicken & Vegetables

Screams out Sunday arvo roast with the family.

Serves 6

1 chicken (around 1.6kg)	10 thyme sprigs
a selection of your favourite vegetables	I head of garlic
to roast	1 lemon
olive oil	2 rosemary sprigs
salt and pepper	

Preheat the oven to 240°C.

Cover the bottom of a large roasting tray with an assortment of your favourite roasting vegetables, such as potatoes, onion, carrot and pumpkin.

Pour over olive oil and season with salt and pepper.

Scatter 5 of the thyme sprigs and all the garlic cloves over the vegetables.

To prepare the chicken, simply halve the lemon and stuff both pieces into the cavity of the bird.

Stuff the leftover thyme sprigs and both of the rosemary sprigs into the cavity.

Rub the chicken all over with olive oil and season the skin with salt.

Place the chicken on top of the vegetables and place into the oven.

Immediately reduce the temperature of the oven to 190°C and cook for 1 hour and 20 minutes.

You may need to remove the chicken a few times to agitate the vegetables during the cooking time.

After the chicken is cooked, leave to rest for a further 20 minutes before carving.

Andy's Chilli Tuna Pasta Bake

This is a massive hit with my family and was also a hit with my housemates in the MasterChef house.

Serves 4

200g kalamata olives, pitted

1 tbs olive oil

1 onion, finely diced

2 cloves garlic, finely sliced

3 anchovies, finely chopped

1 x 425g can tuna in brine, drained

½ cup chopped parsley

5 thyme sprigs, leaves removed

¼ Thai chilli, finely diced with seeds in

¼ cup baby capers

2 x 400g cans of tomatoes

1 cup pasata (Italian tomato sauce)

juice of 1 lemon

1 tbs thickened cream

salt and pepper to taste

400g packet penne pasta

1 cup parmesan cheese, grated

Crush the olives and slice them in half. On the stove top, heat a frying pan that you can also use under a griller. Add the oil, and sauté the onion, garlic and anchovies over a medium heat until they are translucent.

Meanwhile, bring a large pot of water to the boil.

Add the tuna to the onion and garlic, along with the olives, parsley, thyme and fresh chilli. Sprinkle in the capers and stir for 2 minutes. Add the canned tomatoes, pasata and lemon juice and stir. Add ¼ cup of water and simmer for 5 minutes.

Add the cream and cook for 2 minutes until it is incorporated into the mixture. Add salt and pepper to taste and turn off the heat.

Cook the pasta according to the packet directions, preferably till al dente. Drain the pasta and add it to the frying pan. Mix through sauce. Sprinkle grated parmesan over the top.

Preheat the griller for a few minutes. Place the whole pan under the griller for 5 minutes until the cheese is melted and brown. Serve immediately.

Beer Battered Fish

This has been a favourite of mine since I was a little kid.

Serves 2

    2L canola oil
    6 flathead tails, skinned
    ½ cup plain flour for dusting

    BATTER
    1½ cups plain flour
    1 tbs sea salt flakes
    300ml beer

In a large saucepan, heat the canola oil to 180°C.

To make the batter, combine the flour and salt in a bowl. Pour the ice cold beer into the flour and stir vigorously with a fork until there are no lumps. It should be the consistency of paint. (After this you can consume any leftover beer.)

Dust the fish in flour. Shake fish to remove all the excess flour and dunk in the batter so the fish is well covered. Fry the fish in hot oil until golden brown. Serve with fries, or Rosemary Hand-Cut Chips (see recipe in this section).

Butterflied Barbecued Lamb Leg

This dish is perfect for a dinner party with family and friends.

Serves 6

3 cloves garlic
2 rosemary sprigs
5 thyme sprigs
zest of 2 lemons or limes
¼ cup olive oil
1.5kg butterflied leg of lamb
mint leaves to garnish

Roughly slice the garlic and take the rosemary and thyme off their sprigs.

Mix together the garlic, herbs, zest and olive oil.

Rub the mixture over the leg of lamb, cover and leave to marinate for a few hours, overnight if possible.

Place the lamb on the barbecue, skin side down, on a medium to high heat.

Turn the leg over and cook for around 7 minutes.

Put the hood down on the barbecue and cook for a further 10 minutes for medium rare (or longer for meat to your taste, depending on the heat of your barbecue).

Take the lamb off the barbecue and leave in a warm place for 10 to 15 minutes to rest.

Carve the meat and serve it on a chopping board. Garnish with mint leaves. Serve with Greek-style yoghurt, lemon wedges or sauce of your choice (see Sauces section). You can also serve in pitta pockets.

Indian Lamb Curry

Your kitchen will be filled with the aromas of India.

Serves 4

600g lamb shoulder
salt and pepper
¼ cup olive oil
4 cloves
6 allspice berries
2 cardamom pods
1 cinnamon stick
2 bay leaves
1 onion, peeled and chopped
2 cloves garlic, chopped
2cm piece of ginger, peeled and grated
2 tsp ground cumin
1 tsp ground coriander
½ tsp cayenne pepper
2 tbs tomato paste
2 cups chicken stock
425ml coconut cream
8 chat potatoes, quartered
2 cups basmati rice
fresh coriander to garnish

Cube the lamb, season with salt and pepper and rub with 2 tablespoons of oil.

In a deep casserole dish or pan, brown the lamb cubes in 2 tablespoons of oil and set aside.

In the same pan, heat 1 tablespoon of oil and cook the cloves, allspice, cardamom, cinnamon and bay leaves for about 2 minutes, until fragrant.

Add the onion, garlic and ginger, and cook for 5 minutes until onion is soft. Add the cumin, coriander and cayenne and stir.

Mix in the tomato paste and cook for 2 minutes. Return the lamb to the pan and add the stock. Bring to a simmer, cover and simmer for one hour.

Uncover and add the coconut cream and potatoes. Cook for a further 20 minutes.

Meanwhile, cook the rice according to the packet directions, preferably steamed.

Serve the lamb on top of the steamed rice.

Garnish with fresh coriander.

Mid-Week Beef Curry

This mild curry is perfect for the whole family, including the kids.

Serves 4

750g chuck steak, cut into 2cm chunks
¼ cup olive oil
1 tbs coriander seeds
1 tbs cumin seeds
1 tbs fennel seeds
1 brown onion, roughly diced
1 long Thai chilli, finely sliced
2cm piece of ginger, peeled and finely diced
2 cloves garlic, finely sliced
1 tbs mustard seeds

2 tsp turmeric powder
1 tbs tomato paste
2 cups beef stock
juice of 2 lemons
salt and pepper
steamed basmati rice, coriander and natural
    yoghurt, to serve

Brown the meat over a medium to high heat in a large saucepan with half the oil and set aside. Do not clean the saucepan!

While the meat is browning, toast the coriander, cumin and fennel seeds in a dry pan over a medium to low heat for 2 minutes or until the spices become fragrant.

Place the spices into a mortar and pestle and grind until they are a fine powder.

In the same saucepan in which you browned the meat, sauté the onion, chilli, ginger and garlic in the remaining oil over a medium to low heat, until the onions have become translucent.

Add the spice mix from the mortar and pestle, the mustard seeds and the turmeric powder and fry until the mustard seeds start to pop.

Return the meat to the saucepan and stir until every piece of meat is covered in the spice mix. Add the tomato paste and the stock to the saucepan and stir to combine. Stir in the lemon juice and bring to the boil. Reduce to a low simmer.

Cover pan with a lid and cook the curry for 90 minutes or until the meat starts to soften.

Cook uncovered for a further 15-20 minutes. This will allow the sauce to thicken. Add salt and pepper to taste.

Serve with steamed basmati rice, a dollop of natural yoghurt and a sprinkle of fresh coriander leaves.

Roast Beef with Winter Vegetables

Serves 4

400g beef eye fillet, trussed

6 thyme sprigs

4 King Edward potatoes, peeled and cut in
  quarters

4 parsnips, halved

3 tbs olive oil

4 cloves garlic, unpeeled

salt and pepper

8 baby onions, peeled

8 baby carrots, peeled

4 beetroots, halved (around a golf ball size)
  and peeled

HORSERADISH & CRÈME FRAÎCHE SAUCE

½ cup crème fraîche

1 tbs horseradish, or according to taste

zest and juice of ½ a lemon

1 tsp seeded mustard

salt and pepper to taste

Prepare your beef. If it isn't already trussed, tie beef in a roll with string, and marinate it in 3 thyme sprigs and olive oil (or ask your butcher to truss the fillet if you're unsure how to do it). Marinate for a minimum of one hour.

Preheat the oven to 180°C.

Place the potatoes and parsnips into a roasting pan with some olive oil, 2 unpeeled garlic cloves, 3 thyme sprigs and a generous sprinkling of salt and pepper.

Toss in all of the other vegetables and coat well in the olive oil. Place in the oven for around 40 minutes or until they are just cooked through and browned. Turn vegetables once or twice while they are cooking.

To cook beef, bring a non-stick pan to a medium heat. Lightly oil the pan and add the beef, browning on all sides.

Place the beef in the oven for 15 minutes for medium rare (add another 5 minutes for medium).

Make the horseradish and crème fraîche dressing by mixing all the ingredients together in a small bowl until well combined.

This is where your taste will come into play. If you want a big punch of horseradish add more or if you want a really zesty dressing add more lemon juice.

Remove beef from the oven and leave to rest, covered with foil, for 15 minutes.

Serve the beef with the winter vegetables on the side and a dollop of crème fraîche dressing on each plate.

Slow Braised Beef Casserole

Serves 4

½ cup plain flour

2 tbs salt flakes

1kg chuck steak, cut into 2cm chunks

¼ cup olive oil

1 large brown onion, roughly diced

3 cloves garlic, roughly chopped

1 large carrot, cut into chunks

1 celery stalk, chopped into 2cm pieces

4 thyme sprigs, leaves removed

2 rosemary sprigs, leaves removed

2 tbs marjoram leaves

juice of 1 lemon (optional)

1 cup red wine (merlot is best)

1½ cups beef stock

1 can (400g) diced tomatoes

Preheat the oven to 150°C.

Mix the flour and 1 tablespoon of the salt together and dust the beef pieces in the mix.

Shake any excess flour from the beef and brown in batches in a flame-proof casserole dish over a medium heat with half the olive oil. Do not overcrowd the pan. You want the meat to brown and not stew.

Once the beef is browned, set aside in a bowl.

Add the remaining olive oil to the casserole dish and brown the onion, garlic, carrot and celery over a medium heat. This should take around 3 to 5 minutes.

Return beef to the dish, add the thyme, rosemary and marjoram leaves. Stir for around a minute.

Add the lemon juice, red wine and stock.

This is when you should make sure all the brown bits are scraped off the bottom of the casserole dish and are now part of the stock.

Add the tomatoes, stir, and bring to the boil.

Season with remaining salt.

Cover with a lid and place in the oven for 2 hours or until the meat is falling apart.

Serve casserole with Pomme Puree (see recipe in this section).

Pomme Puree

Take a little time to make the perfect mashed potato that will go with everything from steak to beef cheeks.

Serves 4

6 large desiree potatoes, skin on
60ml milk
60g butter, cubed
salt to taste

Cover the potatoes in cold, salted water in a saucepan and bring to the boil. Simmer for 15-20 minutes or until the potatoes can easily be pierced with a knife and are really soft.

Drain the potatoes and peel them while they are hot. Cut each potato in half and place face down into a sieve or colander. Put a tea towel over the potatoes and push them through the sieve into the saucepan. I also find it easy to push them onto plastic wrap placed on a board and gather them up from there.

Return potatoes to the saucepan over a low heat.

Warm the milk until tepid. Then add to the potatoes with the butter. Beat into the potato with a spoon, season with salt and serve.

Chunky Beef Pies

Last night's casserole makes the perfect filling for these pies.

Makes 12 pies

Slow Braised Beef Casserole
6 large sheets shortcrust pastry (or see recipe
    on page 154)
1 egg, beaten

Prepare the Slow Braised Beef Casserole (see recipe in this section) .

In the last half hour of cooking, take the lid off the casserole and reduce mixture over a low heat until it becomes quite thick. You can use any leftover beef casserole, but reduce the liquid by heating until it becomes thick

Preheat the oven to 180°C.

Line the base and sides of each hole of a large 12-hole non-stick muffin tray with shortcrust pastry so the pastry overhangs the top of the tray. Using a cookie cutter, cut out the pastry to fit the tray.

Spoon some of the mixture into the pastry cases until each is almost full.

Place a pastry lid on top and crimp the base and top together so that the pie is completely sealed.

Brush with egg and bake for around 25-30 minutes or until the pastry is brown and crispy.

Beef Ribs in Kecap Manis, Soy, Ginger, Garlic & Chilli

Wait until you try these....

Serves 4

4 beef short ribs

salt and pepper to taste

3 tbs vegetable oil for the rub

4 shallots, diced

4 cloves garlic, diced

4cm piece of ginger, peeled and diced

1 red chilli, diced

2 stalks lemon grass, chopped
(white part only)

¼ cup kecap manis

2 tbs soy sauce

1L chicken stock (plus extra if required)

8 chat potatoes, cut in half

8 cherry tomatoes, cut in half

juice of 2 limes

2 cups basmati rice

½ cup coriander leaves, to garnish

Season the beef ribs with salt and pepper and rub with oil. Heat the remaining oil in a large deep frying pan and brown the ribs. Remove the ribs and keep the oil hot.

Sauté the shallots, garlic, ginger, chilli and lemon grass in the oil over a medium heat for 3 minutes or until fragrant.

Return the ribs to the pan and add the kecap manis and soy sauce. Bring to a simmer and add the chicken stock. Simmer and cover for 2½ hours, checking every 20 minutes. Be sure to add more stock to stop the ribs from sticking.

Add the potatoes and simmer uncovered for a further 15 minutes. Add the tomatoes and simmer for a further 2 minutes. Add lime juice.

Cook the rice according to the packet directions. Serve ribs with steamed rice and garnish with coriander leaves.

Greek Salad

Few things beat sitting on the beach in the middle of summer eating a fresh Greek salad.

Serves 4

DRESSING
2 tbs olive oil
juice of 1 lemon
1 tbs oregano, dried
2 tsp salt
2 tsp cracked pepper

15 cherry tomatoes, halved
100g kalamata olives
150g fetta cheese, cut into 1cm cubes
2 Lebanese cucumbers, sliced
1 red capsicum, deseeded and cut into 1.5cm
   squares
$1/3$ red onion, finely sliced

To make dressing, whisk the olive oil and lemon juice until combined. Add the oregano, salt and pepper and whisk until incorporated.

Combine all other ingredients in a bowl and toss together. Add the dressing and give a final toss.

Serve immediately.

Rosemary Baked Hand-Cut Chips

Serves 2

3 large Sebago potatoes
2 tsp olive oil
2 tsp salt
2 tsp cracked black pepper
2 rosemary sprigs
3 cloves garlic, skin on

Preheat the oven to 160°C.

Slice the potatoes thinly, to around a 2mm thickness. (You may want to use a mandoline for this.)

Toss the potatoes in the oil making sure both sides are well coated.

Sprinkle a generous amount of salt and pepper over both sides of the potatoes.

Lay the potatoes on baking paper on a baking tray and drizzle with olive oil.

Pull the leaves off the rosemary sprigs and scatter over the potatoes. Add the cloves of garlic.

Place the tray in the preheated oven for 15 minutes.

After 15 minutes, turn the chips over and continue to bake for a further 10 minutes or until they are golden and crisp. Discard the garlic to serve.

If the chips start to brown too heavily around the outside, reduce oven to 150°C.

Honey Carrots

Serves 2

1 bunch baby carrots

½ red onion, cut into 4 wedges

2 cloves garlic, halved

1 tbs clarified butter (ghee)

1 tbs olive oil

3 thyme sprigs, leaves removed

1 tbs honey

juice of ½ a lemon

salt and pepper to taste

1 tbs water if needed

Cut off the tops and around 1cm from the base of each carrot.

Thoroughly wash the carrots under cold water, removing any dirt and grit.

Give the carrots a quick peel.

In a non-stick frying pan, sauté the carrots, onion and garlic in the butter and olive oil, over medium to low heat until carrots are just tender.

Add the thyme leaves, honey and lemon juice.

Toss the carrots around, season with salt and pepper and serve immediately.

You may need to add some water if the honey becomes too sticky.

Chicken Caesar Salad

Serves 4

3 slices sourdough, cut into 2cm cubes

2 cloves garlic

5 thyme sprigs

2 tbs olive oil

8 pancetta slices

2 chicken thigh fillets, seasoned with salt and
   pepper

1 cos lettuce

50g parmegano regiano, or parmesan, shaved

2 eggs, softly poached

DRESSING

7 anchovy fillets

½ tbs white wine vinegar

1 tbs Dijon mustard

1 egg yolk

½ clove garlic, minced

1 tsp lemon juice

1 cup extra virgin olive oil

salt and pepper to taste

Preheat the oven to 150°C.

Place the sourdough cubes onto an oven tray with the garlic cloves and thyme sprigs. Drizzle with 1 tablespoon of olive oil and toss to coat the bread. Place in preheated oven for 10-15 minutes or until the bread has dried out and is lightly browned.

Place the pancetta slices over the croutons and continue to cook for another 10 minutes until the pancetta is nice and crispy.

Meanwhile, pan fry the seasoned chicken thigh fillets in the remaining olive oil over a medium heat for 4 minutes each side, depending on the size of the thigh, or until cooked through. Roughly chop once cooked.

To prepare the lettuce, cut the end off the cos around 3cm from the base of the root. Peel the leaves away from around the stem and wash any dirt from the leaves in ice cold water. Thoroughly dry the leaves.

To make the dressing, place the anchovies, white wine vinegar, mustard, egg yolk, garlic plus the lemon juice, into a food processor and blitz. Once ingredients are processed together, add the olive oil at a steady drizzle through the top of the food processor while motor is running.

Once the olive oil has been emulsified, add the salt and pepper, to taste.

To assemble the salad, place a bed of cos leaves on a platter or board, then layer over the croutons, roughly chopped chicken pieces, pancetta shards and the shaved parmegano regiano.

Top with the softly poached eggs and a generous drizzle of the dressing.

Scones

Who doesn't love the smell of the kitchen when scones are in the oven?

Makes 12 scones

2 cups self-raising flour
2 tsp baking powder
2 tsp fine salt
75g butter
125ml milk, plus extra for brushing
extra flour for dusting

Preheat oven to 200°C.

Sift the flour, baking powder and salt together in a large mixing bowl.

Mix in the butter. My Nan used to incorporate the cold butter into the mixture by rubbing it into the flour with her fingertips until it resembled breadcrumbs. A few pulses of a food processor will get the same result.

Create a well in the middle of the flour mixture and add the milk. Stir with a knife to blend the milk into the flour until it comes together.

Turn the dough out onto a floured benchtop, lightly knead and roll out until it's 2½cm thick.

Using a round cutter, cut the dough into portions and make into balls with your hands.

Place the scones on a lined baking tray 1cm apart and lightly brush with the extra milk.

Bake for 15 minutes until golden brown. Serve with jam and whipped cream.

COOKING FOR MY FRIENDS

Feeding my friends was one of the hardest but most satisfying jobs I have had to do. The task of having a few of the boys around for beers and a feed doesn't sound too tough but when you take into consideration how fussy my mates are about what they eat, I had a job on my hands. I'm happy to say that after years of weaning them onto different tastes and flavours I now have a bunch of foodie mates who I can feed anything to, or take anywhere for dinner.

It all started with me hosting regular weekend gatherings, but that soon escalated. The numbers grew and grew until sometimes I'd be catering for around 20. As the barbecues started out pretty simply, so did the food, with basic share food dishes such as Tempura Prawns and Salt and Pepper Squid being the norm. As the numbers grew, so did my creativity, and I started to challenge our palates together.

One day my friends Anthony and Letetia asked me to cater for their wedding and without even asking for details, I threw myself into the challenge without hesitation. They had in mind a tapas-style menu for about 60 guests. Putting on a brave face, I accepted with some trepidation.

It was then down to the menu. I decided on three different dips on arrival, followed by seven different tapas throughout the night. It featured dishes from this book such as the Smoked Salmon Crostini, Barbecued Prawns with Salsa Verde and the Mediterranean Chicken Skewers.

With the menu sorted it was time for a test run as I had no idea how many portions of each different dish I would need to create to satisfy 60 guests. There was also the budget, the timing – the list went on. I invited around 20 of my buddies over for a trial run and away I went. The wedding guest list had since increased to 90 so I was seriously under the pump.

I felt I had it all sorted until MasterChef decided to schedule my first interview the day before the wedding – my prep day! I raced back from Sydney, stopping to pick up my produce, and started to prepare for the wedding at 3pm. Without sleeping that night, I managed to get everything prepared. I'm happy to say that the wedding was a massive success. The bride and groom could not have been happier with the quality of the food I served that day.

This huge event had to be one of the most stressful but satisfying things I have experienced – MasterChef included! You might ask why? When you think about the logistics of not only catering for a wedding, but your friends' wedding, by yourself, without the luxury of a safety blanket in the shape of Gary, George or Matt, it is still one of my biggest achievements.

Cooking for my friends has always been about one thing: having fun. I'm happy to say after everything that has happened, I'm still holding those weekend gatherings. But hey, now I have written this book, some of my mates might even cook for me!

Thai Fish Cakes

Packed full of flavour. You can use any firm fleshed fish.

Makes 16 fish cakes

500g fresh salmon, deboned, skinned (or
  canned salmon)

1 tbs kecap manis

2 tbs coriander leaves

1 tbs palm sugar, grated (or brown sugar)

1 egg

1 tsp salt

2 kaffir lime leaves

zest and juice of 1 lime

2 spring onions, finely chopped

150ml sunflower oil

RED CURRY PASTE

1 red chilli

1 lemongrass stalk, finely sliced (white part
  only)

2 shallots

1 tbs ginger, peeled and grated

2 cloves garlic

Make the red curry paste by blending all the ingredients, or pounding in a mortar and pestle to make one large tablespoon. (You can also use prepared red curry paste.)

Cut the salmon into chunks and mix with the kecap manis, coriander, palm sugar, egg, salt, kaffir lime leaves, red curry paste, lime juice and zest. Use a food processor or potato masher to blend ingredients until well combined – chunky but not pureed. Stir through the spring onions.

Divide into 16 portions and roll and flatten into patties.

Heat the oil in a frying pan to a medium heat. Fry the patties in batches for about 2 minutes on each side or until golden brown. Drain on absorbent paper.

Serve with a dipping sauce such as Nam Jim, or Sweet Soy Dipping Sauce (see Sauces section) or Sambal (see Seafood Salad with Green Mango, Coconut & Sambal).

Whole Baked Snapper with Chilli, Garlic, Ginger & Coriander

Watch your mates smile when you open the bag and they see what's inside.

Serves 2

2 lemons

1 whole baby snapper

1 x 3cm cube ginger, peeled and finely sliced

1 clove garlic, finely sliced

1 long red chilli, finely sliced

½ cup coriander leaves

2 tbs olive oil

salt and pepper to taste

Preheat the oven to 200°C. Slice 1 lemon into thin slices. Score the snapper every 2cm along the skin to the bone, on each side of the fish.

Mix together the ginger, garlic, chilli and coriander leaves.

On a large piece of aluminium foil, spread out 4 slices of the lemon, followed by half of the herb mixture, half of the olive oil and salt and pepper.

Place the snapper on top of the mixture.

Top the snapper with the remaining herb mix, 4 lemon slices and the remaining olive oil.

Season with salt and pepper and the juice of the remaining lemon.

Wrap the snapper loosely in the foil, keeping some air in the bag so the snapper can steam.

Bake in the oven for 35-40 minutes.

The Crispiest Skin Pork Belly

Serves 4

1 x 750g piece of pork belly
olive oil
salt and pepper

Preheat oven to 240°C.

Score the skin of the pork at 1cm intervals, taking care not to go too far into the flesh. Coat both sides of the pork with a generous amount of olive oil. Season the flesh side with both salt and pepper.

On the skin side, rub a generous amount of salt over the skin, making sure to get some salt down inside the score marks.

Place the pork on a wire rack, skin-side up, over a baking tray filled about halfway with water. Place into the oven to cook for 45 minutes.

Reduce the oven temperature to 150°C and cook for a further 2 hours.

This pork belly goes well with Pear & Fennel Salad (see recipe in the next section) or Honey Carrots (see recipe in Cooking for My Family section).

Note Starting the pork at 240°C will ensure the crackling is nice and crisp.

Tempura Prawns
with Sweet Soy Dipping Sauce

True Japanese tempura is white, but I like it golden in colour and extra crunchy.

Serves 4

24 raw medium-sized king prawns
2L canola oil for deep frying
1½ cups plain flour
½ cup cornflour
¼ cup sea salt flakes, plus extra to season
3 tsp freshly ground black pepper
1L chilled soda water
ice

SWEET SOY DIPPING SAUCE

1 birdseye chilli, finely chopped with seeds
    left in
½ clove garlic
1 tbs ginger, minced
½ cup kecap manis
2 tbs soy sauce
juice of 2 limes
zest of 1 lime
¼ cup picked coriander leaves

Keep your soda water in the fridge and make sure it is really cold. It's important that the soda water is as cold as you can get it, without freezing. Peel and devein prawns, removing heads but leaving the tails intact.

Heat the oil in a large deep frying pan over a high heat until it reaches 180°C.

Mix one cup of the plain flour with the cornflour in a bowl. Add the sea salt and black pepper.

Add 3 cups of chilled soda water, and 10 ice cubes to the flour and mix. Stir it with 2 chopsticks quickly, in a figure of 8 motion until it resembles thick paint. Don't over-mix the flour.

Dust the prawns in the remaining plain flour. Treating each one individually, shake the flour and drag it through the wet tempura batter. Place each one into the hot oil for a minute or until golden and crispy. Don't overcrowd the oil. It's best to do about 2 prawns at a time.

Place prawns on paper towels when they come out of the oil and season immediately with salt flakes. Combine all ingredients for Sweet Soy Dipping Sauce and serve on the side.

Note For tempura vegetables, use small broccoli and cauliflower florets, and carrot pieces.

Smoked Salmon Rilettes

This is up there as one of my favourite dishes.

Serves 6-8

300g piece of salmon fillet, skinned and
   boned
2 sourdough baguettes
1/3 cup extra virgin olive oil
200g smoked salmon, chopped
2 tbs baby capers, finely chopped
1 eschalot, finely chopped
zest of 2 lemons
½ bunch dill, finely chopped
½ bunch chives, finely chopped

200ml crème fraîche
cornichons (small pickled cucumbers) and
   lemon cheeks to serve
salt and freshly ground black pepper to
   season

Place fresh salmon in a heavy-based saucepan. Pour 1L boiling water over fish and cover with a tight-fitting lid. Stand for 30 minutes to gently poach.

Meanwhile, heat a char-grill pan or barbecue to medium-high heat. Brush bread with oil and char-grill for 2 minutes on each side or until lightly charred. Set aside.

Remove cooked salmon from water and pat dry. Remove and discard skin. Flake flesh into a large bowl and cool completely. Add smoked salmon, capers, eschalot, lemon zest, herbs and crème fraîche. Stir until just combined. Season with salt and freshly ground black pepper.

Serve rilettes with bread, cornichons and lemon cheeks.

Barbecued Prawn Skewers & Salsa Verde

Perfect summer barbecue material.

Makes 6 skewers

24 large green prawns, peeled, deveined and
    with tails on
6 pre-soaked bamboo skewers or steel ones
2 tbs extra virgin olive oil
salt and pepper to taste
lemon wedges, to serve

SALSA VERDE
1 cup flat leaf parsley leaves
½ cup basil leaves
¼ cup mint leaves
2 tbs baby capers
5 anchovy fillets
½ cup extra virgin olive oil
¼ cup red wine vinegar
juice of 2 lemons
salt and pepper to taste

Thread the prawns onto the skewers, through one side of the tail, out the other and then through the body of the prawn.

Repeat until 3-4 prawns have been threaded onto each skewer.

Drizzle with olive oil and season with salt and pepper.

On a hot barbecue or char-grill pan, grill the prawns for around 90 seconds each side or until the prawns change colour and are just cooked through.

To make Salsa Verde, finely chop all the herbs, capers and anchovy fillets and place in a bowl.

Add the olive oil, red wine vinegar and lemon juice.

Season with salt and pepper to taste.

Spoon Salsa Verde over the prawns and serve with lemon wedges.

Smoked Salmon & Avocado Mousse Crostini

This is a classic combination of flavours – quick and easy to prepare for multiple numbers of people.

Serves 6

2 ripe avocados
juice of ½ a lemon
1 tbs olive oil, plus extra for drizzling
salt and pepper to taste
1 small baguette
250g smoked salmon
½ bunch fresh dill

Preheat oven to 180°C.

Place the avocado, lemon juice and olive oil in a bowl and, using a stick blender, blend until a smooth paste. Season with salt and pepper.

Slice the baguette into ½cm rounds, place on a baking tray, and cook in the oven for 3 minutes or until lightly toasted.

Once toasted, spread approximately 1 teaspoon of avocado mousse over the toasted crostini.

Place the smoked salmon on top of the avocado mousse. Top with a sprig of fresh dill and a drizzle of olive oil.

Salt & Pepper Squid

This was a favourite of mine and Ben's in the MasterChef house while having a beer and watching the footy.

Serves 4

4 medium-sized squid tubes and tentacles
2L sunflower oil
¼ cup salt flakes, plus extra to sprinkle
¼ cup black pepper
2 cups plain flour
½ cup cornflour
1 tbs cayenne pepper
lemon wedges, to serve
Nam Jim Dipping Sauce (see Sauces)

To prepare the squid, cut the tubes into 2½ x 5cm pieces. On the inside of the flesh, make score marks approximately 3mm apart in a crisscross pattern, making sure you don't break the skin.

Preheat the oil to 180°C in a large, deep frying pan.

Using a mortar and pestle, pound the salt and pepper to a coarse grind.

Mix the flours, salt and pepper mix, and the cayenne until well combined.

Dust each piece of squid with the mixture, shaking off the excess flour mix.

Fry in hot oil for 1 minute. Remove and place on absorbent paper and season with the extra salt flakes while still hot.

Serve with lemon wedges and Nam Jim Dipping Sauce or Tartare Sauce (see Sauces section) and an ice cold beer.

Mussels in White Wine

When you need a quick and inexpensive seafood fix, mussels are the go!

Serves 2

2 cloves garlic, chopped

2 shallots, diced

50g butter

100ml dry white wine

16 mussels, de-bearded

60ml cream

1 large tomato, deseeded and diced

½ bunch flat leaf parsley, chopped

juice of 1 lemon

freshly cracked black pepper

In a large saucepan, sauté the garlic and shallots in half the butter. Cook until transluscent.

Add the wine and simmer for 2 minutes. Add the mussels and place the lid on the pan. Shake the pan and cook on a low heat for 3 minutes.

Add the cream and shake the pan again.

Add the tomato, parsley, lemon juice and remaining butter and shake again.

Pour the mussels and sauce into a large bowl, add cracked pepper and serve with crusty bread.

Popcorn Chicken with Lime Mayo

Such a great bar snack!

Serves 4

2L sunflower oil
500g chicken tenderloins
1 cup plain flour
3 eggs
100ml milk
3 cups breadcrumbs
salt

LIME MAYO

100ml Kewpie Mayo is the best, or other good
     quality mayonnaise
juice and zest of 1 lime

Preheat the oil in a saucepan to 180°C.

While the oil is heating, combine the Lime Mayo ingredients in a bowl and mix well together to form a cream. Place in the fridge while you make the Popcorn Chicken.

Chop the chicken tenderloins into 1½cm cubes and dust in the flour.

Lightly beat the eggs together with the milk. Shake the excess flour from the chicken and dunk the cubes in batches into the egg mix.

Drain and roll the chicken pieces in the breadcrumbs. Repeat until all the chicken has been crumbed.

When the oil is hot, deep fry the chicken for about 2 minutes or until it is browned and cooked through.

Remove the chicken and place on paper towels. Season with salt while hot.

Serve with Lime Mayo on the side.

Mediterranean Chicken Skewers with Coriander Yoghurt

Makes 8 skewers

1 chicken breast

1 red capsicum

1 medium zucchini

1 red onion

5 thyme sprigs, leaves removed

2 cloves garlic, finely sliced

2 tbs olive oil

8 pre-soaked bamboo skewers

lemon wedges, to serve

CORIANDER YOGHURT

¼ cup of coriander leaves, chopped

½ cup natural yoghurt

juice of ½ a lime

Chop the chicken breast into 2cm chunks. Cut the capsicum lengthwise into two cheeks. Remove the seeds and membrane. Chop into 2cm squares. Slice the zucchini thinly. Peel the onion and chop into 6 wedges, separating them into individual onion layers.

Mix all the remaining ingredients together with the vegetables in a bowl and marinate for 12 hours or overnight. Soak the skewers in water for a few hours or overnight, to prevent burning.

To make the Coriander Yoghurt, mix together the coriander, yoghurt and lime juice to taste.

Skewer a piece of chicken on each skewer, followed by capsicum, zucchini and red onion. Repeat until each skewer has two pieces of chicken and two pieces of each vegetable.

Heat a barbecue hot plate or char-grill pan to sizzling. Cook each skewer for 3-5 minutes on each side of the skewer until the chicken has cooked through. Serve with Coriander Yoghurt and lemon wedges.

Asian-Style Lamb Ribs

See how long these take to disappear.

Serves 4 or more as a sharing plate

1 kg lamb short ribs
¼ cup fresh coriander leaves to garnish

MARINADE
2 tbs palm sugar
2 tbs soy sauce
2 tbs kecap manis
2 tbs honey
2 tbs peanut oil
2 tbs tamarind
1 tsp ground coriander
1 clove garlic
1 tsp ginger, peeled and grated
1 tsp salt
juice of 2 limes

Blend all the marinade ingredients in a bowl. Place lamb in a large glass dish and drizzle the marinade over. Cover and refrigerate overnight.

Preheat oven to 150°C. Place the lamb ribs on a wire rack in the oven and slow roast for 1½ hours. Garnish with fresh coriander leaves.

Mediterranean Lamb Sliders

Makes 16

800g lamb mince

½ bunch coriander leaves, finely chopped

2 cloves garlic, finely diced

1 tbs ground coriander seeds

1 egg

½ cup breadcrumbs

2 shallots, finely diced

1 bunch mint leaves, finely chopped

2 tsp chilli flakes (optional)

zest of 2 lemons

1 tbs salt

1 tbs black pepper

1 cup vegetable oil for frying

2 red capsicums

2 zucchinis

salt and pepper to taste

1 tbs olive oil

Tzatziki (see Sauces section)

mini sourdough rolls to serve

Combine all ingredients except for the oil, capsicum, zucchini and tzatziki in a mixing bowl and mix thoroughly using your hands, for approximately 3 minutes.

Divide the mixture into 16 even portions and roll into balls. Make into oval-shaped burger patties.

For the roast capsicum, char the skin of the capsicums over an open flame of your gas burner, until the skin is totally blackened, or place in an oven preheated to 240°C until the skin is black all over.

Place the blackened capsicum into a bowl and cover immediately with plastic wrap.

Leave the capsicum to steam for 15 minutes, after which the skin should easily come away from the flesh.

To char-grill the zucchini, slice zucchini lengthwise into 3mm strips.

Coat with olive oil and season with salt and pepper.

Char-grill on a griddle pan over a medium heat until there are char marks on the zucchini. Turn over and repeat.

Heat oil in a medium-sized frying pan. Flatten each patty slightly with a slicer and fry each patty for 2 minutes on each side.

Serve the burgers on a some mini sourdough rolls with roasted red capsicum, char-grilled zucchini and a dollop of Tzatziki.

Pork & Fennel Sausage Rolls

I've had my fair share of bad pies and sausage rolls. These are not them.

Makes 18

6 cloves garlic, diced

6 shallots, diced

1 red chilli, diced

1 fennel bulb, diced

1 tbs vegetable oil

¼ cup fennel seeds

4 thyme sprigs, leaves removed

1 apple, preferably Granny Smith, grated

1 carrot, finely grated

1kg pork mince

1 tbs salt

1 tbs pepper

40g breadcrumbs

4 sheets ready-made puff pastry

1 egg for egg wash

Preheat the oven to 180°C.

In a large frying pan, sauté the garlic, shallots, chilli and fennel in the oil over a medium heat for 3 minutes. Add 2 tablespoons of the fennel seeds and thyme leaves. Stir for one minute until aromatic.

Add the apple and carrot and cook for a further 3 minutes. Allow the mixture to cool.

In a bowl, combine the pork mince with the vegetable mixture. Add salt, pepper and breadcrumbs. Using your hands, mix thoroughly for about 3 minutes to bring the mixture together.

Roll out the pastry and cut into 6 long rectangles, 15 x 30cm.

Divide the filling into 6 even portions and roll each portion into a 30 x 3cm log.

Beat the egg in a dish. Place each pork mince log in the centre of each pastry rectangle. Brush one long edge with the egg wash. Lift up the non-washed edge and roll it firmly over the filling to join with the egg wash side underneath.

Cut each roll into 3 even pieces and place on baking tray. Brush the top of each roll with egg wash and sprinkle with remaining fennel seeds. Bake for 30 minutes or until golden brown.

Serve with a relish of your choice.

I first met Ben at the MasterChef auditions and we got on immediately. Ben has introduced me to Mexican flavours which I love. I'll let him take over from here.

Andy has a unique way of looking at food. Not bound by tradition or culture, he is able to push the boundaries because he is unaware of them, and most importantly this means there is only ever one thing on his mind – flavour. During the competition Andy was literally a sponge, any conversation we had about food would be a learning experience, every challenge a chance to try something new. His ability to pair flavours and develop ideas eventually shone through. I love discussing food and recipe ideas with Andy as we bring out the best in each other and the food always tends to be better when we have had fun cooking it together.

Andy and I share a very similar background, which is one of the reasons we developed such a strong bond during MasterChef. Just as Andy did, I spent most of my summers on the water fishing with my Dad and mates. The fishing obviously led to cooking and eating seafood which means we both have a particular love for this key ingredient.

Mexican food is all the rage at the moment and it's no wonder when you consider that Mexican food culture introduced the world to chocolate, corn, chillies, tomatoes, vanilla, avocado and guava. Andy and I are just scratching the surface of Mexican food, which is one of the oldest cuisines, but one of the newest trends. It is the perfect food for sharing which I think is one of the reasons we like it so much. It's packed full of flavour, healthy and makes great use of seafood, another reason we are so into it. My love of Mexican food was developed at a young age through the Mexican taco kits you get in supermarkets. During summer holidays tacos were a staple diet for me, so Mexican food was always connected to long hot summer days and good times playing backyard cricket, swimming at the beach and fishing off the jetty.

As my culinary interests and skill developed, I started to venture away from the packet Mexican and to experiment with more varied flavours and ingredients.

The recipes in this section are a great introduction to Mexican food, if you like what you see and taste then let your imagination run wild and come up with your own recipes. Some of the recipes require authentic Mexican ingredients like chipotle chillies and Masa Harina cornflour. These ingredients are starting to become more common and many are available online.

Ben Milbourne

Chicharron Guacamole

Serves 4

2 avocados, diced

1 tbs green chilli, diced

juice of 1 lime

1 tsp salt flakes

¼ red onion, finely diced

2 tbs coriander leaves, chopped

1 large tomato, deseeded and diced

1 cup of crumbled pork chicharron (pork
    scratching/crackling)

100g corn chips

Place the avocados, chilli, lime juice, salt and onion in a bowl and roughly mash together. Stir in the coriander leaves, tomato and chicharron. Serve with corn chips.

Pineapple & Chilli Salsa

Serves 4

½ fresh pineapple
1 long red Thai chilli
½ Lebanese cucumber
½ cup coriander leaves
juice of 2 limes
salt and pepper

Remove skin from pineapple, cut out eyes, slice into 1½cm cubes, and place into a medium sized serving bowl.

Deseed and julienne the chilli. Cut the cucumber in half and deseed with a spoon and slice into 3mm pieces on the diagonal. Mix in with coriander, pineapple, add the lime juice and salt and pepper to taste.

This salsa is great with fresh seafood and ceviche.

King Fish Carpaccio with Mexican Vinaigrette & Salsa

Serves 4

200g king fish or snapper loin

1 tsp sea salt flakes

juice of 2 lemons

juice of 2 limes

1 green chilli, diced

2 coriander roots

20g palm sugar (or brown sugar)

1 tsp salt

1 clove garlic, diced

2 shallots, diced

1 tsp coriander seeds

1 tbs olive oil

salt and pepper

½ cup fresh cress, picked, to garnish

SALSA

½ cucumber, deseeded and finely diced

½ tomato, deseeded and finely diced

½ avocado, deseeded and finely diced

½ shallot, finely diced

Slice the kingfish or snapper loin with a very sharp knife into 2mm slices onto a plate. Season with salt and cover.

Combine lemon juice, lime juice, chilli, coriander root, sugar, salt, garlic, shallot and coriander seeds in a blender or food processor and process until smooth. Let it sit for 15 minutes for the flavours to infuse. Strain, reserving the juice and set aside.

To make the vinaigrette, add 1 tablespoon of olive oil to strained juice and season with salt and pepper to taste. Mix together the salsa ingredients in a bowl.

Fan the fish pieces out on a plate. Spoon the salsa over the fish and garnish with cress. Spoon over the vinaigrette and serve.

Taco Baja, Pickled Jalapeno & Chipotle Coleslaw

Serves 4

TORTILLAS: MAKES 8 (OR USE
READY-MADE TORTILLAS)

1 cup Masa Harina

1 cup warm water

1 tsp sea salt

PICKLED JALAPENO

½ cup white vinegar

½ cup caster sugar

3 jalapeno peppers

BATTER

1½ cups plain flour

1 tbs sea salt

300ml ice cold beer

1L vegetable oil for frying

½ cup plain flour for dusting

8 flathead tails, or any firm white fish

salt to taste

Chipotle Coleslaw (see recipe overleaf)

lime wedges, to serve

1 bunch coriander leaves

To make tortillas, mix all the ingredients together to form a smooth dough. Rest for 30 minutes. Divide into 8 portions. Roll each portion into a golf ball and using a rolling pin, roll out to 2mm thick. Heat a non-stick or heavy-based frying pan. Dry fry each tortilla for 2 minutes on each side and then set aside on a tea towel or absorbent paper. Stack the tortillas with baking paper, separating each one until you are ready to assemble.

To pickle the jalapenos, bring the vinegar and sugar to the boil. Cut the jalapenos into 2-3mm slices and place in a heatproof bowl. Pour the vinegar and sugar mixture over the jalapenos and allow to steep for 5 minutes. Drain and set aside.

To make the batter, combine the flour and salt in a bowl. Pour 300ml of ice cold beer into the flour and stir vigorously with a fork until there are no lumps and it is the consistency of paint.

Heat the oil to 180°C in a deep frying pan. Dust the flathead tails in flour and then cover them in the beer batter and deep fry for 2-3 minutes. Drain on absorbent paper and season with salt.

Assemble the tacos by placing 1 tablespoon of chipotle coleslaw on the tortilla, then the flathead tail, then 3 jalapenos. Sprinkle with coriander and serve with lime wedges.

Note Masa Harina can be bought online. It is a Mexican flour which is made from corn which is treated with lime.

Chipotle Coleslaw

Serves 4 as a side salad

100g Kewpie Mayo is the best, or other good
    quality mayonnaise
1 tsp chipotle seasoning
zest of 1 lime, plus juice of ½ a lime
¼ red cabbage, shredded
1 carrot, finely sliced
¼ white cabbage, shredded
1 medium sized raw beetroot, finely sliced
salt to taste

Mix the Kewpie Mayo with the chipotle seasoning. Add the lime juice and zest. Place remaining vegetables in a serving dish. Fold the Kewpie Mayo through the mixture.

Season with salt to taste and serve.

Popcorn Prawns Tostada

This is Ben's take on a classic Mexican dish, using prawns.

Serves 4

12 green prawns, peeled and deveined
tempura batter (see Tempura Prawns recipe in
　　this section)

TOSTADA: MAKES 24
1 cup yellow cornflour (Masa Harina is best)
1 cup warm water
1 tsp sea salt

AVOCADO PUREE
2 avocados, peeled and deseeded
juice of 1 lime
15g palm sugar, grated
1 tbs crème fraîche
salt and pepper to taste

CORN SALSA
1 cup fresh corn kernels
1 tbs butter
salt and pepper to taste
2 tbs pumpkin seeds

1L vegetable oil for frying
1 cup fresh enoki mushrooms, trimmed
1 bunch coriander

Cut the prawns into 3 even pieces. Dust with flour and cover with tempura batter.

In a large, deep pan, heat vegetable oil to 180°C. Deep fry the prawns for 30 seconds or until cooked through.

To make tortillas, mix all the ingredients together to form a smooth dough. Rest for 30 minutes. Divide into 8 portions. Roll each portion into a golf ball and using a rolling pin, roll out to 2mm thick.

Using a 5cm cookie cutter, cut into rounds.

Heat a non-stick or heavy-based frying pan. Dry fry each tortilla for 2 minutes on each side and then set aside on a tea towel or absorbent paper for 10 minutes.

Deep fry tostadas in batches until crisp. Remove from oil.

To make the avocado puree, blitz the avocado, lime juice, palm sugar, crème fraîche, salt and pepper in a blender and pass through a fine sieve. Set aside.

To make the corn salsa, sauté the corn kernels in butter for 5 minutes, season and set aside. Dry toast the pumpkin seeds in a heavy-based frying pan and mix with the corn kernels.

Rinse enoki mushrooms, pat dry and deep fry whole for 1 minute or until brown. Place on absorbent paper and season with a pinch of salt.

Lay out each tostada on serving plates. Top with 2 teaspoons of avocado puree, corn salsa, 3 prawn pieces each, a sprinkle of enoki mushrooms and a coriander leaf.

Note Keep leftover tostadas in an airtight container. You can also substitute the tostadas for a good quality, deli-style corn chip.

A NEW DIRECTION

The final section in my book. As the name suggests, this is the path I have taken with my food both during and after season four of MasterChef. I felt my cooking improved dramatically from the time I entered the house. I learnt every day, but there was something about the trip to Italy that made me look at food in a whole new way. Before we boarded the plane, I felt as though every time I cooked I was struggling to have a clear vision of what my food was meant to look like prior to serving. I came back from Italy and felt like, from then on, I was always going to produce a 'cracking' dish.

In this section, I have featured some of my favourite and most successful dishes from the competition. Funny that! I couldn't resist including two fish pies in my book as I feel they are totally different meals, both in taste and texture. I have also included my now well-known Modern Seafood Basket, but with a few changes. Although it received a 10 and two nines from the judges, I feel it still needed to be refined to make it perfect.

In saying this, my favourite dish that I cooked in the competition was the Braised Beef Shin. To hear the comments from the judges is something I'll never forget.

I encourage you to have a go at each dish. If I was able to reproduce Christine Manfield's 'Gaytime Goes Nuts' in the finale, when I hadn't ever made caramel, ice-cream or honeycomb, there is no reason why you can't perfect every dish in my book.

Even after a trip overseas, meeting many of the world's top chefs and learning from my fellow competitors, the thing I'm still unable to put my finger on is what type or style of cook I am. At the moment I'm content with still experimenting with flavours and textures. I feel there is no need to pigeonhole myself to a cuisine before I travel the world and experience them firsthand. I think the most exciting thing is that I'm still only 24 years-old and have my whole life to work these things out. There are exciting times to come and I hope you're just as excited as I am to see what happens next.

New Basics

The skills I've learnt have changed the way I cook now. I can't give you all those lessons, but here are a few of the things that I learnt about in the beginning that set me on my path to a new way of cooking.

My favourite piece of equipment is my chef's knife. Get yourself a good knife – 25cm is a good size. Try and sharpen your knives regularly on steel or get them sharpened; do that every time and you will notice a difference.

A Pressure Cooker

I can't tell you enough how much I love this piece of equipment and feel as though all home cooks should have one amongst their pots and pans. With a limited amount of time to cook in most of the MasterChef challenges, a pressure cooker took a dish which needed to be braised for three hours and achieved the result in under an hour.

It's as simple as browning your meat and vegetables in your pressure cooker, adding your liquid, popping on the lid and cooking under pressure for 45 minutes to an hour. Once the meat is tender, strain away the sauce and reduce it in a pan until it's at the right consistency.

This is perfect for the home cook. I know when cooking for my family I had a window of around an hour in which I had to have dinner on the table. Using a pressure cooker I can now achieve the perfect soup, curry or braise in a fraction of the time.

Confit

This is another technique that I assumed took hours to achieve. But with the right research into cooking time and temperatures a confit is easily achieved. I also urge you to have a crack at this as the technique can lift your standard dish through the roof in terms of taste and texture. The original confit is cooking a protein, generally duck, in its own fat. In recent times animal fat has been replaced with olive oil. The process involves submerging the protein or vegetabe in olive oil and cooking at a low temperature for a longer period of time. For example, an 80g salmon fillet cooked for 15 minutes at 45°C. The reason for this, is that oil separates from water and by surrounding the ingredient in oil, it ensures all moisture remains inside. Don't be alarmed by the use of oil during confiting. As you are cooking the protein or vegetable at low temperature the oil has no chance of penetrating into its flesh and creating an oily product. Give it a go.

The Sweet–Sour–Salt Crunch

This is something we talked about a lot on MasterChef, and all the incredibly experienced chef judges and guests would often mention this. This is the flavour of the dish when it is served – there has to be a balance between the sweet and sour, and there has to be a scale of salt taste. The crunch is when it all comes together – if you can get these flavours happening together in a scale that balances, you have a really interesting and new dish!

Pickling

I discovered pickling as a technique during MasterChef. I always thought for something to be pickled it had to be placed in a brine for a long period of time and was used to preserve the life of the ingredient. While this can be the case, I soon found out that pickling is so simple, takes no time at all and gives food a whole new character.

Take pickled ginger for instance. We have all seen it in Japanese restaurants and it takes just a few minutes to achieve this product, which tastes so much more fresh and flavoursome than the stuff out of a jar.

Simply bring a standard pickling liquid – equal quantities of white vinegar and white sugar – to the boil. Once all the sugar has dissolved, place your finely sliced ginger into the pan. Take the pan off the heat and allow the ginger to steep in the liquid until it cools.

Ginger can be substituted for all sorts of vegetables and fruits, such as cucumber, mushrooms or jalapeno peppers to name a few.

Once you have mastered the standard pickle, get creative and play around with your pickling liquid. Start to flavour your pickling liquid with herbs and spices.

Pickling takes no longer than 10 minutes and can add a whole new dimension to your dish.

Pastry

Another technique I was too scared to tackle prior to MasterChef was making pastry. I now realise that shortcrust pastry can be made by anyone, regardless of cooking experience. I've given you the option in all these recipes of buying shortcrust ready-made. But if you can make it yourself you will add a lot of flavour and texture to your pies and tarts.

Simple Shortcrust Pastry

Makes enough for 12 small pies or 1 family-size pie

250g plain flour
125g unsalted butter, chopped into cubes
1 cold egg, lightly beaten
1 tbs cold water

Simply place the flour and butter into a food processor and blitz until the mix looks similar to breadcrumbs.

Continue to blitz and add the egg and a touch of the water until the mixture starts to form large clumps.

Take the mixture out of the food processor and knead until the dough comes together. Wrap in plastic wrap and rest in the fridge for at least half an hour.

This pastry can be rolled out and used for the base of your quiche, pie or even tarte tartin.

Schezuan Pepper School Prawns with Roast Garlic Aioli

Serves 4

²/₃ cup Schezuan peppercorns

1 tbs salt flakes, plus extra to season

½ cup plain flour

½ tbs cornflour

750g raw small or medium sized school
   prawns

2L vegetable oil for frying

ROAST GARLIC AIOLI

1 head garlic

1 bottle of mayo (Kewpie Mayo is the best, or
   other good quality mayonnaise)

To make the Roast Garlic Aioli, preheat oven to 180°C. Roast garlic head in the oven for 30 minutes until the cloves are soft. Remove cloves from their skins and mash until they become a fine paste. Fold garlic paste through the mayo until smooth and well combined. Set aside.

In a medium pan, dry roast the Schezuan peppercorns until fragrant.

Using a mortar and pestle, pound the roasted Schezuan peppercorns and the salt flakes to a course grind.

In a separate bowl, mix the flours together and add the salt and Schezuan peppercorn and salt mix.

Peel and devein the prawns, leaving the tails on. Preheat the oil to 180°C. Toss the prawns through the flour mix until well coated, and fry in batches in the hot oil for approximately 1½ minutes or until super crunchy.

Remove from the oil and place on absorbent paper. Season with the extra salt flakes while still hot. Serve with Roast Garlic Aioli.

Oysters with Japanese Dressing

Serves 4

JAPANESE DRESSING
½ cup caster sugar
½ cup white vinegar
6cm ginger, peeled and finely sliced
1 tsp soy sauce
3 tsp mirin
2 tsp rice wine vinegar
¼ long red chilli finely diced, with seeds left in
½ clove garlic, finely chopped
zest of 1 lime
¼ bunch of coriander leaves, finely chopped

12 oysters in their shells
coriander leaves, finely chopped

To make the Japanese dressing, bring the sugar and white vinegar to the boil and pour over the ginger. Set aside to cool for 5 minutes.

Combine the soy sauce, mirin, rice wine vinegar, chilli, garlic, lime zest, coriander and pickled ginger. Leave the dressing to infuse for 5 minutes then divide the dressing evenly amongst the freshly shucked oysters.

Top with finely chopped coriander.

Red Onion Tarte Tatin

I still get a buzz when these turn out perfectly onto the bench.

Makes 16 tarts

50g unsalted butter

1 tbs olive oil

1kg red onions, roughly sliced

6 thyme sprigs, leaves removed

2 cloves garlic, roughly chopped

1 tbs caster sugar

1 tbs balsamic vinegar

1 tbs red wine vinegar

300ml canola oil

16 sage leaves

3 sheets ready-made puff pastry

2 egg yolks for brushing

100g goats cheese

salt and pepper to season

Preheat the oven to 180°C.

In a large heavy-based saucepan melt the butter and the olive oil over a medium to low heat, until the butter starts to foam.

Add the onions, thyme and garlic and sweat off for about 5 minutes, stirring occasionally. Add the sugar and vinegars and give the onions a good stir.

Reduce the heat to low and continue to cook the onions for another 20 minutes, stirring every few minutes so the onions don't stick to the pan.

While the onions are cooking, heat the canola oil in a small saucepan to 180°C. Throw the sage leaves into the oil and fry until they are crispy. This won't take long! Drain on a paper towel and set aside.

Once the onions have cooked, grease a 16-hole non-stick muffin tray with cooking spray. Cut discs of pastry to the diameter of the muffin tray.

Place a spoonful of the onion mixture into each hole, and top with a disc of pastry. Lightly brush the pastry with egg yolk and repeat the process until the tray is full.

Bake in the oven for 15 minutes or until the pastry is golden and crispy.

Turn out onto the bench and top with some of the goats cheese and crispy sage and season with salt and pepper.

Confit Salmon with Sweet Soy Dressing

After learning how to prepare confit on MasterChef I adapted a recipe and created this using salmon. You will need a cooking thermometer for this recipe.

Serves 4

½ cup caster sugar

½ cup white vinegar

6cm piece of ginger, peeled and julienned

500ml extra virgin olive oil

4 x 80g pieces salmon, skinned and boned

2 tbs sesame seeds, toasted

1 small baby fennel shaved, plus the fronds

SWEET SOY DRESSING

½ cup kecap manis

2 tbs soy sauce

juice of 2 limes

1 clove garlic, minced

2 kaffir lime leaves, julienned

2 tbs whole coriander leaves, plus extra to garnish

1 red chilli, sliced

Pickle the ginger by bringing the sugar and white vinegar to the boil. Once the sugar is dissolved, pour over the ginger and set aside to cool.

Heat the olive oil to 46°C in a pan. You will need a cooking thermometer as the temperature is crucial. Place the salmon in the oil in the pan so it is totally submerged. Keep the salmon in the oil at this temperature for 15 minutes. Remove the salmon from the oil and gently pat dry and roll in toasted sesame seeds.

For the dressing, pour kecap manis, soy sauce, lime juice, garlic, kaffir lime leaves, coriander and chilli into a bowl and mix until well combined.

To serve, spoon some of the dressing into a shallow bowl and place the salmon in the middle. Scatter around some shaved fennel, and the fronds, with the coriander leaves and ginger.

Note You may have some pickled ginger left over to use in another recipe.

Seared Scallops with Corn Puree & Currant Vinaigrette

Serves 4

4 fresh corn cobs

¼ head cauliflower

500ml chicken stock

1 tsp shallots, finely diced

juice of 1 lemon

1¼ tbs currants

2 tbs olive oil

1 tbs butter

1 tbs cream

16 scallops

salt and pepper to taste

Slice kernels from the corn cobs. Cut the cauliflower into mini florets. (You will need around 6-8 per serve).

In a pan, bring the chicken stock to the boil. Cook the corn kernels in the stock for 10 minutes. Strain the corn and reserve the stock.

Bring a separate pan of water to the boil. Add a pinch of salt and blanch the cauliflower for 1 minute. Drain and set aside at room temperature.

Make the vinaigrette by mixing the shallots, lemon juice and currants together. Set aside. Before serving, whisk in 1 tablespoon of olive oil.

Place the corn in a blender with 1½ tablespoons of the reserved stock, the butter and the cream. Puree. Pass the corn puree through a fine sieve.

Drizzle the remaining oil over the scallops. Heat a frying pan to a high heat, add the scallops and cook each side for 30 seconds until scallops are browned and caramelised, being careful not to overcook them.

To serve, smear each plate with the corn puree. Top with the scallops and cauliflower florets. Spoon over the vinaigrette and season to taste.

Popcorn Pork Spare Ribs with Moroccan Yoghurt Dressing

When Ben and I received a mystery box at a recent cooking demo, we came up with this.

Serves 4, or more as a shared dish

5 pork spare ribs	MOROCCAN YOGHURT DRESSING
1½ cups plain flour	1 tbs cumin seeds
1 tbs sea salt flakes	1 tbs coriander seeds
1 tbs cracked black pepper	½ cup natural yoghurt
2L canola oil	juice of 1 lemon
½ cup pepitas	
1 punnet enoki mushrooms	

Trim the pork spare ribs of any skin and excess fat. Chop the pork into 1.5 cm cubes.

Mix the flour, salt and pepper together. Dust the pork pieces in the flour mix until they are well coated in the flour.

In a large, deep frying pan, heat the canola oil to 180°C. Deep fry the pieces of pork, in batches, in the hot oil for around 2-3 minutes or until the pork is just cooked through. Place onto paper towels and season the pork with salt while it is still hot.

Toast the pepitas in a dry pan over a medium heat until they just start to brown.

Make the dressing: toast the cumin and coriander seeds in a dry pan over a medium heat until they become fragrant. This should take around 2-3 minutes. In a mortar and pestle, pound the seeds until they are a fine powder. Sift through a fine sieve.

Add the coriander and cumin seeds to the yoghurt, according to your taste. Add the lemon juice.

Toss the mushrooms and pepitas together with the pork. Finally, scatter some fennel fronds over the top as a garnish.

Serve with the Moroccan Yoghurt Dressing. You can also serve with Pear and Fennel Salad (see recipe in this section).

Chicken Parma with Roasted Tomato Sugo & Prosciutto Shards

My take on an old classic. Once you've tried this, you won't go back to the pub and order parma chicken.

Serves 4

1 loaf stale sourdough

1 tbs olive oil

5 thyme sprigs

2 cloves garlic

4 chicken breasts

3 eggs, lightly beaten

¼ cup milk

½ cup plain flour

2L canola oil

8 slices prosciutto

100g grated parmesan

fresh cress to garnish

ROASTED TOMATO SUGO

500g roma tomatoes

100ml olive oil, plus extra for drizzling

4 cloves garlic

1 large brown onion, finely diced

10 thyme sprigs plus a handful of leaves

juice of 1 lemon

1 tbs salt

1 tbs black pepper

½ cup parsley leaves, roughly chopped

Preheat the oven to 150°C.

Slice the sourdough into 1½cm slices and then into cubes about 1½ x 1½cm. Place the bread cubes on an oven tray and drizzle with 2 tsp olive oil. Scatter the thyme sprigs over the bread, and place garlic cloves onto the tray. Toss the bread cubes around so each is coated in the olive oil. Place the bread into the oven for 20 minutes or until the bread is dry and lightly browned. Remove from oven. Blitz the bread cubes in a food processor until you have a rough crumb.

Make the Roasted Tomato Sugo. Slice the tomatoes into quarters. Lie them on an oven tray and drizzle with olive oil. Throw in the thyme sprigs and 2 garlic cloves. Roast for 45 minutes or until completely soft. Slice the 2 remaining garlic cloves. In a fry pan sauté the onion and garlic over a medium to low heat until the onion is translucent. Add the thyme leaves and stir. Add the chopped roasted tomatoes, and discard the roasted garlic and thyme. Simmer for 2 minutes. Add salt and pepper to taste. Stir in the lemon juice and 100ml olive oil. Simmer for 3 minutes and stir in fresh parsley.

With a meat mallet, beat the chicken fillets until they are an even thickness.

In a bowl, mix the egg and milk until well combined. Dust the chicken in flour, shake off any excess, then dip the chicken into the egg mixture. Remove any excess egg mix, then coat the chicken in the breadcrumbs.

You may want to dip the chicken back in the egg mix and breadcrumbs for a double crumbed coating. In a large saucepan, preheat the canola oil to 180°C and fry chicken in batches until crisp and golden. Remove from oil and set aside to drain on paper towels.

Preheat the oven to 160°C. Place the prosciutto in between two sheets of baking paper and 2 trays to keep it flat and place in oven for 10 minutes. Remove from oven and leave to cool and crisp up.

To serve: place a generous amount of the Roasted Tomato Sugo over the deep fried chicken breast and top with grated parmesan. Place under the grill until the cheese is golden.

Top with the prosciutto shards and garnish with cress.

Crispy Skin Duck with Witlof

Serves 4

ORANGE SAUCE
200g brown sugar
150ml water
100ml kecap manis
juice of 3 limes
3 cinnamon sticks
4 star anise
3 oranges, peeled and cut into 1cm rounds

4 x duck breasts
salt flakes
1 tbs caster sugar
100ml water
4 witloff, cut into quarters
2 red onions cut into wedges
3 cloves garlic
1 tbs olive oil
salt and pepper to taste
fresh cress to garnish

Preheat oven to 180°C.

To make the sauce, dissolve the brown sugar in the water over a medium heat in a saucepan and simmer for 3 minutes. Add the kecap manis and lime juice and simmer for 6 minutes. Add the cinnamon sticks and star anise and simmer for another 3 minutes. Add the oranges and take off the heat and allow to infuse for no longer than 5 minutes.

To cook the duck, score the skin in a crisscross fashion and season with salt flakes. Place skin side down in a dry cold pan. Over a medium heat cook the duck until the skin is golden and crisp – approximately 5 minutes. Transfer the duck to a preheated oven and cook for 6 minutes until the duck is medium rare (cooking time will vary depending on the size of the breasts). Rest the duck under foil for 10 minutes.

Add sugar to 100ml of water and bring to the boil in a medium frying pan. Once the sugar has dissolved, place the witlof cut-side down in the pan, cover with a lid and cook for 10 minutes or until witlof softens and starts to brown.

Place red onions in a roasting pan with garlic, oil, salt and pepper and cook in the oven for 15 minutes or until softened.

Slice the duck breasts into 6 pieces. To serve, create a bed of witlof and red onion in the bottom of a shallow bowl. Place the duck pieces on top. Spoon a generous amount of the orange sauce over the duck and garnish with cress.

Beef Cheeks with Pomme Puree

Serves 4

4 beef cheeks (or beef brisket)

¼ cup plain flour

2 tsps each of salt and pepper

2 tbs olive oil

1 carrot, roughly chopped

2 rashers bacon, diced

1 celery stalk, roughly chopped

1 onion, diced

2 cloves garlic, diced

1 cup red wine

1L veal (or beef) stock

2 bay leaves

2 sprigs rosemary

4 sprigs thyme

¼ cup orange juice, or to taste

salt and pepper to taste

Pomme Puree

(See recipe in Cooking for My Family
section)

Dust beef cheeks in flour, salt and pepper. Heat oil to medium in a large saucepan and brown the beef cheeks on each side for approximately 5 minutes. Remove beef cheeks and set aside.

In the same pan, sauté carrot, bacon, celery, onion and garlic over a medium heat for 5 minutes. Return beef to the pan and add red wine and simmer slowly until it reduces by half.

Add the stock, bay leaves, rosemary and thyme. Cover and simmer for 2-3 hours until the beef is tender.

Half an hour before beef is ready, prepare the Pomme Puree according to recipe (see recipe in Cooking for My Family section).

Remove the rosemary and thyme. Add orange juice to taste to reinvigorate the sauce.

Serve each beef cheek a bed of pomme puree with a generous amount of sauce.

Seafood Salad with Green Mango, Coconut & Sambal

The fresh combination of flavours makes this a tasty treat at any time of the day. The sambal can be used with anything, especially seafood.

Serves 4 as a starter, 2 as a main dish

½ cup shredded coconut

1L vegetable oil for frying

500g barramundi or firm fish fillet

1 green mango

1 bunch mint

1 bunch Thai basil

SWEET AND SOUR SAMBAL

2 tbs coconut or peanut oil

6 cloves garlic

4 shallots

2 dried chillies, soaked

3 anchovies

10g galangal or ginger, peeled

40g palm sugar, grated (or brown sugar)

juice of 1 lime

30ml kecap manis

To make the sambal, heat the coconut oil in a frying pan and add the garlic and shallots and fry until golden. Add the chilli, anchovies and galangal. Heat for 3-5 minutes. Remove to a mortar with a slotted spoon, leaving the oil in the pan. Pound the ingredients to a paste and return to the pan. Cook in the coconut oil for 2 minutes. Add the sugar, kecap manis and lime juice and cook until it becomes a jam-like consistency, approximately 5 minutes. Set aside to cool.

Preheat the oven to 180°C. Scatter the shredded coconut on an oven tray and toast for 3-5 minutes.

Heat the vegetable oil to 180°C. Cut the fish into 8 pieces and deep fry in the vegetable oil until golden. Drain and set aside.

Shred the mango and chop the green herbs.

To serve, place the fish pieces in a bowl. Add the toasted shredded coconut. Mix and garnish with the green herbs and mango. Finally, dollop with the sweet and sour sambal.

Roast Sweet Potato Salad with Chorizo, Red Onion & Goats Cheese

Serves 4 as a side salad

1 clove garlic, finely sliced

2 red onions, peeled and cut into wedges

¼ cup olive oil

salt and pepper to taste

1 large sweet potato

1 chorizo sausage

juice of 3 lemons

¼ cup pumpkin seeds

60g creamy goats cheese

Preheat oven to 180°C.

In a small baking dish, place the garlic, onion wedges with a 1 tablespoon of olive oil and salt and pepper to taste. Place in the oven for 20 minutes or until softened.

Peel the sweet potato and slice lengthwise into 1½cm pieces. Cut into strips diagonally, approximately 5cm in length. Line a separate small baking dish with the strips of the sweet potato. Drizzle with 1 tablespoon olive oil and salt and pepper to taste. Place in the oven and bake for 15 minutes.

Cut the chorizo sausage into ½cm slices and place in a cold frying pan, with 1 tablespoon olive oil. Heat slowly until heat reaches medium, and fry for 5 minutes until the sausage is golden brown. Turn off the heat and allow the sausage to sit in the oil and infuse for 10 minutes. Remove the chorizo from the frying pan, strain and keep the oil to one side. Mix the reserved oil with the lemon juice and stir. Add salt and pepper to taste.

Heat a frying pan to medium and pan roast the pumpkin seeds until light brown for about 3 minutes, shaking the pan during frying.

Break the goats cheese into chunks. Remove the sweet potato and onions from the oven. To serve, pile the sweet potato in the bottom of a dish, add the onions and sausage, sprinkle with the pumpkin seeds and the goats cheese. Drizzle salad with the strained oil.

Pear & Fennel Salad
with Moroccan Yoghurt Dressing

A fresh Middle Eastern salad that works brilliantly with steamed fish, poached chicken or Popcorn Pork.

Serves 4

2 Beurre Bosc pears, peeled

1 baby fennel bulb

500ml sunflower oil

1 cup enoki mushrooms, trimmed

2 radishes, finely sliced

½ cup pitted dates, roughly sliced

2 tbs toasted pepitas

½ cup fennel fronds

Moroccan Yoghurt Dressing
    (see recipe in Sauces section)

Heat the sunflower oil to 180°C. Deep fry the mushrooms until crispy and brown. Season with salt while hot.

Slice the pears and set aside. On a mandoline or with a sharp knife, finely shave the fennel and set aside.

Toss the pears, fennel, radish and dates together. Serve with a sprinkle of pepitas and top with a sprinkle of the enoki mushrooms and fennel fronds.

Serve with Moroccan Yoghurt Dressing.

I decided to include just a few of the recipes that I prepared on MasterChef here in the book. These were the dishes that I made under pressure alongside my team and we all feel we created something really special. I am personally proud of these recipes and they look fantastic when they are served.

You may think they are difficult to do, but really it's question of taking the time and reading the recipe. I have included some substitute ingredients and methods for the home cook who may not be as adventurous as us when we were on MasterChef. I encourage you to try them out, after all I was once a novice home cook as well.

Modern Seafood Basket

My take on an Aussie classic. Didn't score too badly with the judges either!

Serves 4

6 small marron
   (or yabbies if you can't find marron)
salt to taste
2 desiree potatoes, peeled
1L vegetable oil, for frying
2 tbs baby salted capers, rinsed, patted dry
2 tbs wakame seaweed
3 purple radish, sliced into 2mm-thick rounds

OYSTER EMULSION

1 tbs olive oil
3 eschalots, diced
500ml dry white wine
200ml white wine vinegar
4 oysters, plus 6 extra in the shell, to serve
100g cold butter, diced

DEEP FRIED ABALONE

4 abalone (or squid)
½ cup plain flour
2 eggs, lightly beaten
salt and pepper to taste
2 cups Panko breadcrumbs

PAN-FRIED FLATHEAD TAILS

2 flathead tails, about 10cm long
1 cup plain flour
salt and pepper to taste
1 tbs olive oil

Preheat oven to 220°C.

Poach marron in boiling salted water for 3 minutes. Drain and refresh in ice cold water for 3 minutes. Remove head, peel tail, removing gastro intestinal tract, ensuring you keep tail intact.

Make the oyster emulsion. Heat oil in a small saucepan over medium heat, add eschalots and cook until translucent. Add wine and vinegar and simmer until mixture has reduced to 100ml. Strain. Just before serving add 4 oysters and butter to the reduction and blend with a stick blender until foaming and smooth.

Cut potatoes into cylinders using a cookie cutter and slice thinly into rounds using a mandoline. Place on a well-oiled tray, brush lightly with oil and bake in oven until golden and crisp.

Remove abalone from shell, clean and trim and place in freezer until almost firm. Slice thinly, coat in flour, then seasoned egg, then roll in bread crumbs. Heat oil in a deep fryer to 180°C and deep fry the abalone for 90 seconds. Drain on paper towels and keep warm.

Remove the skin from the flathead tails. Coat tails in seasoned flour. Heat olive oil in a large frying pan over medium heat and cook flathead tails on both sides until golden brown Transfer to oven and bake for 2-4 minutes until cooked through and keep warm.

Deep fry capers in hot oil until crisp, drain on paper towel.

To serve, arrange flathead tail, marron, abalone, oysters in shell, wakame seaweed, capers, radish and potatoes on the serving plate. Spoon over oyster emulsion.

Smoked Trout Pie

My first MasterChef mystery box win!

Serves 2

1 smoked trout
20g butter
1 tbs olive oil
1 red capsicum, diced
1 small fennel bulb, fronds reserved and
   broken into small pieces, bulb diced
150ml thickened cream
2 tbs roughly chopped dill, plus extra fronds
   to serve

zest and juice of ½ a lime
3 slices bread
40g parmesan cheese, finely grated

Preheat oven to 200°C.

Remove the trout flesh from the bones, and set aside in a bowl. Place the bones into a medium-sized saucepan and pour over cold water to half-fill the pan. Bring to the boil for 10 minutes to make stock.

Meanwhile, heat butter and oil in a frying pan over low heat and sauté the capsicum and fennel bulb until soft. Strain the stock into a jug; you need approximately 300ml. Add the stock to the capsicum and fennel and simmer until it has reduced by half.

Add the cream and trout and simmer for 10 minutes. Add the dill, lime zest and juice and cook a further 2 minutes.

Place the trout mixture into one pie dish or two individual dishes.

Tear the bread into pieces and place on a baking tray. Place in the oven until golden brown. Scatter the toasted bread pieces on top of the pie and sprinkle with parmesan. Cook under a preheated grill for 2 minutes until golden and the cheese is melted. To serve, top with dill and fennel fronds.

Braised Beef Shin, Pomme Puree, Bone Marrow & Vegetables

Serves 2

BRAISED BEEF SHIN

salt and pepper

½ cup plain flour

2 pieces beef shin

2 tbs olive oil

1 carrot, diced

1 brown onion, diced

2 cloves garlic, finely chopped

400ml red wine

200ml veal stock

1 sprig rosemary

5 sprigs thyme

diced butter, red wine or veal stock, as required

VEGETABLES

50g butter, plus 150g chilled butter, thinly sliced

6 eschalots, peeled

250ml veal stock

6 baby turnips, washed and halved

¼ cup fresh peas

1/3 cup chicken stock

baby cress, to serve

Pomme Puree (See recipe in Cooking for My Family section)

Mix salt and pepper with flour and coat the beef pieces. Heat 1 tablespoon of oil in a heavy-based pan and brown beef on all sides until it has a nice crust. Add carrot, onion and garlic and sauté until well caramelised. Add red wine, veal stock, rosemary and thyme. Bring to the boil, cover and simmer for 2 hours or until beef is tender. You can use a pressure cooker to speed this process up.

Preheat the oven to 180°C.

For caramelised eschalots, melt butter in a frying pan over medium-low, add eschalots and cook until golden. Add veal stock and simmer until nearly all the stock has reduced, approximately 20 minutes.

Place a thin layer of sliced butter in a small saucepan. Lay turnips, flat side down on top of butter. Cook over low heat, adding chicken stock once the butter has melted. Cook until turnips are tender, approximately 30 minutes. Meanwhile, blanch fresh peas in salted water for 2 minutes.

Using a sharp knife, scrape down the sides of the shin bone to remove all excess meat and sinew. Place the bone onto a baking tray and cook for 10 minutes.

Once beef is cooked, pour beef stock into a frying pan and bring to simmer over medium-high heat. Simmer until sauce has reduced, adding butter and little red wine or stock to balance the flavour.

Make the Pomme Puree, see the recipe (see recipe in Cooking for My Family section).

To serve, arrange the beef, turnips, eschalots, peas, bone and Pomme Puree onto serving plate. Scatter over the cress and serve sauce on the side.

$20,000 Fish Pies

On MasterChef we were challenged to cook a dish that would raise money for a charity. These pies generated $20,000 for charity, which I was pretty proud of.

Serves 6

2 sheets ready-made puff pastry

WHITE ROUX
25g butter
20g plain flour

FILLING
1 tbs olive oil
20g butter
1 clove garlic
1 small fennel bulb, diced
1 carrot, diced
1 purple potato, diced
1 thyme sprig, leaves removed
125ml white wine

500ml fish stock
1 tbs chopped chives
1 tbs chopped parsley
salt and pepper to taste
juice of ½ a lemon
20g butter
200ml cream
400g large barramundi fillets, cut into 2cm dice
150g swordfish steaks, cut into 2cm dice
40ml milk to glaze

Preheat oven to 220°C. Grease 6 x ½ cup capacity ramekins.

For roux, melt butter gently in a small saucepan, stir in flour and cook gently for 2-3 minutes, do not allow to colour.

For filling, heat oil and butter in a large frying pan and fry garlic, fennel, carrot, potato and thyme for 8 minutes, or until softened.

Deglaze pan with wine and once most has evaporated, add stock and reduce by two-thirds. Add chives and parsley, salt, pepper, lemon juice and butter. Pour in cream and roux and reduce heat to a simmer. Cook for 6 minutes until thick.

Place 3-4 pieces of fish in each ramekin, spoon 2 tablespoons of sauce over fish.

Cut pastry disks to the size of each ramekin. Place the disks on top of each dish.

Brush pastry with milk and bake for 20-30 minutes until golden and puffed. Serve warm.

DESSERTS

Rosemary Pannacotta with Macerated Strawberries & Gingerbread Crumble

Serves 2-4

120ml thickened cream

120ml full cream milk

3 tbs caster sugar

1 rosemary sprig

2 gold leaf gelatine sheets or 1 tsp powdered
gelatine

6 strawberries

2 tbs red wine vinegar

5 ginger biscuits

Bring the milk and cream to a simmer in a small saucepan over a medium heat, but do not boil.

Add 1 tablespoon of sugar and stir until dissolved. Add the rosemary sprig and take pan off the heat. Let the rosemary infuse for 10 minutes.

After 10 minutes strain the mixture, making sure there are no rosemary leaves left in the mix.

Pour the mixture back into the pan, place over a medium heat and bring to a simmer again.

Add the gelatine and stir until it is fully dissolved.

Cool the mixture over an ice bath, stirring so it doesn't set. Once the mixture has cooled, strain it into your serving glass. Chill the pannacotta in the fridge until it has set firm.

For the strawberries, roughly chop and place in a bowl. Stir through the remaining sugar and the red wine vinegar. Leave the strawberries for 10 minutes, stirring occasionally.

Blitz the ginger biscuits in a food processor until you have a rough crumb.

Once the pannacotta has set, place a few spoons of the strawberries into small glasses or bowls and sprinkle over the gingerbread crumb.

Ben's White Chocolate Mojito Cheesecake with Rhubarb

Serves 4

1 packet oat biscuits

30g butter

1 cup caster sugar

juice of 4 limes

zest of 2 limes

50ml white rum

2 bunches of fresh mint leaves, finely chopped

400g cream cheese

250g mascarpone cheese

180g white chocolate, melted

4 rhubarb stalks, cut into 5cm lengths

2 star anise

1 cinnamon stick

100g roasted pistachios, crushed

whole mint leaves to garnish

In a food processor, blitz the oat biscuits to a crumb. Melt the butter and mix with the biscuit crumbs. Press crumb mixture into the bottom of 4 mojito glasses or one large glass dish.

In a saucepan over a medium heat, place ½ cup sugar and 2 tablespoons of water. Heat until it is dissolved into a syrup and then add the lime zest and juice. Add the rum and mint, reserving some leaves to garnish, and remove from heat. Set aside to infuse and cool.

In a food processor, process the cream cheese and mascarpone until smooth. Strain the sugar syrup and add to the cheese mixture. Add melted white chocolate. Process until well incorporated. Spoon over the biscuit mix and place in the fridge to set, approximately half an hour.

When you are ready to serve, add ½ cup of sugar, rhubarb, star anise, cinnamon stick and 1 tablespoon of water to a pan and bring to the boil. Simmer until the rhubarb is soft. Remove the star anise and cinnamon stick and blend until smooth. Allow to cool and pour the rhubarb sauce over the cheesecake mix.

Garnish with mint leaves and pistachios.

Everyone knows I am still learning the craft of desserts. Luckily meeting guys like Darren Purchase and co means that I am in good hands. In saying that, my book wouldn't be complete without a couple of sweet treats from my buddy Kylie Millar.

When Andy asked if I would write a few dessert recipes for his book I was so chuffed. I thoroughly enjoy cooking with Andy, and to be able to contribute to his book is an honour.

Andy and I first cooked together while filming MasterChef in Italy in the Rome on a Plate episode. It was great! We ventured into the oldest building in Rome, the Pantheon, made (and ate!) gelato, raced around local markets trying to find artichokes and cooked corratella — the insides of lamb. This was our very first experience of cooking offal and although we were not victorious, we felt extremely proud to have had a go at something that was totally out of our comfort zone. That's one of the reasons I enjoy cooking with Andy, he is always willing to have a crack at something a bit different and push the boundaries, whether it is with flavours, techniques or concepts. Andy is laid back and extremely friendly. Along with his competitive spirit he always tries to better himself, which makes for an enjoyable time in the kitchen.

Being creative with food is my passion and something that excites me. I feel like it's a way for me to express myself and have a bit of fun with creating something outside the square. You can bend the rules when it comes to desserts, and for me, as long as you get a smile when you serve the plate up to someone, that's the icing on the cake.

Andy is not only someone I enjoy cooking with, but also a great friend – I feel like I have gained a brother through the course of MasterChef. Eat sweet, dream big.

Kylie Millar

Kylie's Lychee Granita with Caramelised Pineapple & Gin Syrup

Serves 6

1 x 400g can lychees in syrup
juice of 1 lime

CARAMELISED PINEAPPLE
¼ cup caster sugar
½ cup gin
1 pineapple
2 limes, sliced into thin wedges, to serve

Blend lychees, syrup and lime juice in a food processor until pureed. Push through a fine sieve, discarding solids, and freeze. Once frozen, scrape into ice crystals using a fork and return to freezer until required.

Place the sugar and gin into a bowl and stir until dissolved. Peel and slice the pineapple into 1cm rounds. Heat a char-grill pan or barbecue over high heat and brush the pineapple with the sugar mixture. Char-grill or barbecue for 2 minutes each side or until char marks appear.

To serve, slice pineapple into pieces, pop onto a plate, pile granita on top, drizzle with remaining sugar syrup and a wedge of lime.

Kylie's Toasted Coconut & Caramel Parfait Sandwiches

The best thing about a parfait is you don't need an ice cream machine! So no excuses to shy away from giving this a go! Once you've tasted this home-made frozen delight you'll never go back to buying ice cream ever again! I've called this a parfait instead of an ice cream because it is made in a slightly different way to how you usually make ice cream.

PARFAIT

70g shredded coconut

300ml thickened cream

200ml full cream milk

Pinch of salt

190g caster sugar

2 gold strength gelatine leaves, soaked in iced
  water to soften then squeezed to remove
  excess water

2 tbs glucose

60ml water

8 egg yolks

200ml cream, whipped to soft peaks.

BISCUITS

350g softened unsalted butter

350g brown sugar

400g plain flour

CARAMEL SAUCE

150g caster sugar

250ml thickened cream

pinch of salt

Line a 30 x 20cm tin with baking paper.

Preheat the oven to 160°C and on a tray lined with baking paper, place your coconut and toast for 5 minutes or until golden brown. Pour the cream and milk in a saucepan and bring to a simmer. Turn off heat and add the toasted coconut. Leave to infuse for 10 minutes. Pour liquid through a sieve, pushing as much liquid out of the coconut as you can with a spatula, back into the saucepan it came from and heat to a gentle simmer. Reduce heat to low while you make the caramel.

Heat a saucepan over medium heat and divide the caster sugar into two: 140g and 50g. From the 140g, add 1 teaspoon of caster sugar. When it starts to melt gradually add the remaining 140g sugar and stir continuously until all the sugar has melted and is a dark golden brown colour.

Slowly pour the hot cream mixture onto the caramel, while whisking, until the caramel has dissolved into the coconut infusion. Whisk in the gelatine and set aside to cool.

Make the pate bombe.

Add the 50g caster sugar, glucose and water into a small saucepan and bring to the boil. Brush down the sides of the pot with a wet pastry brush to stop the syrup from crystallising. Continue to cook, without stirring, until the temperature reaches 120°C. If you don't have a candy thermometer, heat the liquid until it starts to boil and continue to cook for about 5 minutes, or until the mixture thickens.

Meanwhile, add the yolks into the bowl of an electric mixer and whisk on high until they are light in colour. Once the sugar mixture has reached 120°C, remove from the heat, reduce the speed of the mixer and slowly pour the syrup down the side of the bowl into the yolks. Once the syrup is all incorporated, increase the speed again and whisk until cool.

Gently fold the cooled coconut caramel and pate bomb egg mixture together, then fold in the whipped cream. Pour the parfait into the prepared tin and freeze for about 2 hours until firm.

To make the biscuits, preheat the oven to 180°C.

In an electric mixer, cream the butter and sugar until pale. Turn down the speed of the mixer, add in the flour and mix until just combined.

Divide the mixture into two and roll out between two sheets of baking paper to the same size as the prepared tin (30 x 20cm). You will now have 2 sheets of biscuit dough.

Remove the top sheet of the baking paper before sliding the bottom sheet (with the dough on top) onto a baking tray and bake for 12 minutes or until golden brown. Remove from the oven and cut into rectangles measuring 5 x 10cm while the biscuit is still warm.

Once cut, leave to cool then arrange half of the biscuit rectangles on top of your parfait. This will serve as a guide when cutting.

Remove the parfait from the tin, cut, then flip over by placing a chopping board on top of the parfait. Arrange the other half of the biscuits on top then return to the freezer until ready to serve.

To make the caramel sauce, pour the caster sugar into a heavy based pan over a medium heat. Cook until the sugar has turned a deep golden brown.

Whisk in the cream. If there are any lumps of caramel, whisk the sauce gently over a low heat until they have dissolved. Leave to cool.

To serve, cut the parfait sandwich into slices and pour over the caramel sauce. You can also roll the edged of the sandwich in toasted coconut shreds before serving.

Horseradish and Cremé Fraîche Sauce

SAUCES

Tartare Sauce

This is the classic seafood accompaniment, and when you make it yourself it tastes so much better.

Serves 6

1 tbs gerkins

1 tbs baby capers

1 tbs french eshallots

1 tbs flat leaf parsley

1 cup whole egg mayonnaise

½ tbs dill

1 tbs lemon juice

salt and peper

Finely chop the gerkins, capers, eshallots and parsley.

Place in a bowl with the mayonnaise and mix well. Roughly chop the dill and add it to the mayonnaise. Add the lemon juice and mix well.

Season with salt and pepper and serve with Salt and Pepper Squid, Modern Seafood Basket, or Beer Battered Fish and Chips.

Lime Mayo

This is such a versatile sauce. It goes well with chicken, fish or even pork. If you can get the Kewpie Mayo it's the best, but if you are pushed you can use whatever you have in your fridge.

Serves 4

100ml Kewpie Mayo is the best, or other good
    quality mayonnaise
juice of 1 lime
zest of 1 lime

Combine all ingredients in a bowl and mix well together to form a cream. You can add as much or as little lime as you like. Don't be afraid to experiment with this mayo. A few chilli flakes wouldn't hurt.

Coriander Yoghurt

This simple sauce is quick to make and goes best with curries. Chicken soaks it up.

Serves 6

½ cup natural yoghurt
¼ cup of coriander leaves
juice of ½ a lime

Mix together the yoghurt and coriander. Add the lime juice to taste.

Salsa Verde

This is a fantastic dipping sauce with any seafood.

Serves 6

1 cup flat leaf parsley
½ cup basil leaves
¼ cup mint leaves
5 anchovy fillets
2 tbs baby capers
¼ cup red wine vinegar
½ cup extra virgin olive oil
juice of 2 lemons
salt and pepper to taste

Finely chop all the ingredients and place in a bowl. Add the extra virgin olive oil, red wine vinegar and lemon juice.

Season with salt and pepper to taste.

Moroccan Yoghurt Dressing

This yoghurt sauce is low fat and works well with lamb or chicken dishes.

Serves 4

1 tbs cumin seeds
1 tbs coriander seeds
½ cup natural yoghurt
juice of 1 lemon

Toast the cumin and coriander seeds in a dry pan over a medium heat until they become fragrant. This should take around 2-3 minutes.

In a mortar and pestle, pound the seeds until they become a fine powder. Sift the seeds through a fine sieve.

Add the coriander and cumin mix to the yoghurt according to your taste. You can add as little or as much as you want depending on how strong you want the flavour of the cumin and coriander seeds to be. Add the lemon juice.

Serve with Popcorn Pork Spare Ribs, or any lamb or pork dish.

Sweet Soy Dipping Sauce

Oysters, salmon, chicken, skewers—this sauce is versatile and a staple in our house.

Serves 4

1 birdseye chilli, finely chopped with seeds
    left in
½ clove garlic
1 tbs ginger, peeled finely chopped
½ cup kecap manis
2 tbs soy sauce
juice of 2 limes
zest of 1 lime
¼ cup picked coriander leaves

Combine all ingredients and stir.

Sauce Vierge

Great with seafood, steak and pasta.

90ml olive oil

1 clove garlic, finely chopped

2 anchovy fillets, finely chopped

2 tomatoes, deseeded and diced

juice of ½ lemon

1 tbs parsley leaves, finely chopped

2 tbs basil leaves, finely chopped

salt and pepper to taste

Heat oil, garlic and anchovies into a saucepan on medium until the anchovy has dissolved. Add tomatoes and cook for a minute until warmed through. Remove from heat. Add lemon juice, herbs and salt and pepper.

Roast Garlic Aioli

1 head of garlic

1 bottle of mayo (Kewpie Mayo is the best, or
    other good quality mayonnaise)

Preheat oven to 180°C. Roast garlic head in the oven for 30 minutes until the cloves are soft. Remove cloves from their skins and mash until they become a fine paste. Fold garlic paste through the mayo until smooth and well combined.

The Perfect Steak Compound Butter

This compound butter goes perfectly with any steak. I prefer rib eye but T-bone is also great.

125g butter
1 shallot, diced
2 cloves garlic, diced
½ bunch flat leaf parsley
6 white anchovies
1 tsp white pepper
zest of 1 lemon

Soften butter in a saucepan over a low heat. Increase heat to medium and sauté shallots and garlic until soft. Set aside to cool.

Blanch parsley in boiling water for 30 seconds and then refresh in iced water.

Combine all the remaining ingredients in a food processor and blend until smooth.

Refrigerate until required.

To serve, spoon sauce on top of a steak as soon as it comes off the barbecue.

Tzatziki

Not just for Greek dishes, this sauce is perfect for burgers and is essential for share food.

Serves 4

1½ Lebanese cucumbers, peeled, deseeded
   and finely diced
2 tsp sea salt
500g Greek style yoghurt
4 cloves garlic, roasted
juice of 1 lemon
zest of ½ a lemon
1½ tbs dill, finely chopped
1 tbs extra virgin olive oil

Spread the cucumber slices out on a tea towel. Sprinkle with sea salt and leave the cucumber for 1 hour to extract any moisture.

Depending on the quality of the Greek yoghurt, you may need to place it in some muslin cloth and squeeze out any excess liquid.

On a chopping board, crush the garlic with the back of a knife.

Mix together the yoghurt, lemon juice, zest, garlic, dill and olive oil in a bowl.

Squeeze any excess moisture from the cucumber and add it to the mixture.

Season to taste.

Serve with Mediterranean Lamb Sliders (see Cooking for My Friends section).

Roast Tomato Sugo

The tastiest tomato sauce!

Serves 4

500g roma tomatoes

100ml olive oil, plus extra for drizzling

10 thyme sprigs plus a handful of leaves

4 cloves garlic

1 large brown onion

juice of 1 lemon

1 tbs salt

1 tbs black pepper

½ cup parsley leaves

Preheat the oven to 160°C.

Slice the tomatoes into quarters. Lie them on an oven tray lined with baking paper and drizzle with olive oil. Throw in the thyme sprigs and 2 garlic cloves. Roast for 45 minutes or until completely soft.

Slice the 2 remaining garlic cloves. In a fry pan sauté the onion and garlic over a medium to low heat until the onion is translucent. Add the extra thyme leaves and stir. Add the chopped roasted tomatoes and peeled roasted garlic and simmer for 2 minutes. Add salt and pepper to taste.

Stir in the lemon juice and olive oil. Simmer for 3 minutes and stir in fresh parsley.

Chilli Jam

You can put this on anything!

Serves 4

½ red onion, diced
1 clove garlic, finely sliced
1 thyme sprig, leaves removed
1 tsp olive oil
500g ripe roma tomatoes, deseeded and
   diced
6 long red chillies, chopped
200g brown sugar
40ml white wine vinegar
2 tbs lemon juice
1 tbs fish sauce

1 tsp salt
1 tsp fresh ginger, peeled and grated
fresh coriander, to serve

Sauté the onion, garlic and thyme in olive oil in a saucepan over a low heat until the onion is translucent.

Add the rest of the ingredients and bring to the boil. Lower heat and gently simmer until the mixture thickens and is a jam-like consistency. Remove from heat and allow to cool before spooning into clean jars or serving bowls.

Top with a few coriander leaves.

Basil Gremolata

This goes well with any barbecued seafood, chicken or steak.

Serves 4

1 cup basil leaves
1 cup parsley leaves
zest of 2 lemons
juice of 1 lemon
1 clove garlic
2 white anchovies
1 tbs olive oil
salt and pepper to taste

Combine all the ingredients in a food processor until blended, but not pureed. Add salt and pepper to taste.

Nam Jim Dipping Sauce

This Asian-inspired dipping sauce goes perfectly with seafood, meat or chicken dishes.

Makes 250ml

2 tbs fish sauce
¼ cup vegetable oil
1 red chilli, deseeded and chopped
1 clove garlic, diced
2cm piece of ginger, peeled and chopped
2 tbs palm sugar or brown sugar
juice of ½ a lime
½ bunch of coriander leaves, chopped
1 tbs pineapple juice
1 shallot, diced

Combine all the ingredients in a food processor and blend until smooth.

Hollandaise Sauce

1 shallot, diced

1 tsp butter

½ cup white wine

½ cup white wine vinegar

3 egg yolks

50g clarified butter (ghee)

juice of 3 lemons

2 tbs parsley leaves

salt to taste

1 tsp white pepper

Sauté shallots in butter in a saucepan over a low heat until soft and translucent. Add the white wine and vinegar and simmer until the liquid reduces to around 2 tablespoons. This should take approximately 10 minutes. Strain and keep the liquid only.

A double boiler is best for this next stage. Alternatively, heat water in a saucepan until it is simmering. Float a stainless steel dish in the pan, ensuring dish does not touch the bottom. Add the strained butter and vinegar, with the egg yolks and 1 tbs of hot water. Whisk gently until it forms a ribbon consistency. Do not scramble the eggs.

Remove egg mixture from heat. Warm the clarified butter in the microwave and whisk into the mixture. Add the lemon juice, parsley, salt and white pepper. Use immediately.

This sauces works well with salmon or egg dishes.

Mushroom Sauce

This sauce is perfect for steak or chicken.

Serves 4

2 cloves garlic, finely sliced

1 shallot, diced

1 tbs olive oil

1 tbs butter

4 oyster mushrooms, torn

6 shitake mushrooms, sliced finely into 6

6 Swiss brown mushrooms, sliced finely into 6

3 thyme sprigs, leaves removed

salt and pepper to taste

¾ cup veal or beef stock

juice of ½ a lemon

1 tbs cream

¼ cup chopped parsley leaves

Sauté the garlic and shallots in olive oil and half the butter on a low heat until the shallots soften.

Add the remaining butter, mushrooms and thyme, season with salt and pepper. Increase the heat to medium and sauté until the mushrooms are light brown.

Add the stock and simmer for 5 minutes. Add the lemon juice and the cream and simmer for 3 minutes or until the sauce comes together.

Add parsley and serve.

Index

A Note on Measurements

1 teaspoon (tsp) = 5g/5ml
1 tablespoon (tbs) = 20g
1 tablespoon (tbs) = 20ml
Liquid measures: 1 cup = 250ml (9fl oz)
Solid measures (vary, depending on substance): 1 cup caster sugar = 220g (8oz);
1 cup flour = 150g (5oz); 1 cup white sugar = 225g (24oz)

First published 2012 by New Holland Publishers Pty Ltd
London • Sydney • Cape Town • Auckland
Garfield House 86–88 Edgware Road London W2 2EA United Kingdom
1/66 Gibbes Street Chatswood NSW 2067 Australia
218 Lake Road Northcote Auckland New Zealand
Wembley Square First Floor Solan Road Gardens Cape Town 8001 South Africa
www.newhollandpublishers.com   www.newholland.com.au

A record of this book is held at the National Library of Australia

ISBN 9781742573267

Publisher: Diane Ward
Publishing director: Lliane Clarke
Designer: Tracy Loughlin
Editor: Bronwyn Phillips
Proofreader: Kay Proos
Photographer: Steve Brown Photography
Food stylist: Bhavani Konings
Production director: Olga Dementiev
Printer: Toppan Leefung (China) Ltd

Our thanks to the following stores for their generosity in providing props: Breville • Golden Brown Fox Ceramics •
    Di Lorenzo Tiles • Market Import • Mud Australia • Porter's Paints

Keep up with New Holland Publishers on Twitter: @NewHollandAU
    Facebook and http://www.facebook.com/NewHollandPublishers

10 9 8 7 6 5 4 3 2 1